ENGLISH ROMANTIC POETRY

ENGLISH ROMANTIC POETRY

An introduction to the historical context and the literary scene

KELVIN EVEREST

Open University Press
MILTON KEYNES · PHILADELPHIA

Open University Press
Celtic Court
22 Ballmoor
Buckingham MK18 1XW

and
1900 Frost Road, Suite 101
Bristol, PA 19007, USA

First Published 1990

Copyright © Kelvin Everest 1990

All rights reserved. No part of this publication may be reproduced, stored in a retrieval system or transmitted in any form or by any means, without written permission from the publisher.

British Library Cataloguing in Publication Data
Everest, Kelvin
English Romantic poetry: an introduction to the historical context and the literary scene.
1. Poetry in English, 1745–1837. Romanticism – critical studies
I. Title
821.609145

ISBN 0-335-09298-5
ISBN 0-335-09297-7 (pbk)

Library of Congress Cataloging-in-Publication Data
Everest, Kelvin.
English romantic poetry : an introduction to the historical context and the literary scene / Kelvin Everest.
p.   cm.
Includes bibliographical references (p. 97) and index.
ISBN 0-335-09298-5 (Hb.)   ISBN 0-335-09297-7 (Pb.)
1. English poetry—18th century—History and criticism.
2. English poetry—19th century—History and criticism.
3. Romanticism—England.   I. Title.
PR571.E94   1900
821'.709145—dc20   90-7614   CIP

Typeset by Vision Typesetting, Manchester
Printed in Great Britain by Biddles Limited, Guildford and Kings Lynn

For Faith

Contents

List of illustrations	viii
Preface	ix
Introduction	1
PART ONE: The historical context	7
ONE *Years of revolution: 1775–93*	9
TWO *Years of reaction: 1793–1815*	22
THREE *The post-war period: after 1815*	42
PART TWO: The social relations of the Romantic poets	51
FOUR *Blake, Wordsworth, Coleridge*	53
FIVE *Keats, Shelley, Byron*	59
PART THREE	65
SIX *The literary scene*	67
Conclusion	86
Chronology	88
Bibliography	97
Index	108

List of illustrations

1 William Blake, *Visions of the Daughters of Albion*, 1793, frontispiece — 20
2 James Gillray, 'The Zenith of French Glory; – The Pinnacle of Liberty. Religion, Justice, Loyalty, & all the Bugbears of Unenlightened Minds, Farewell!', 12 February 1793 — 24
3 James Gillray, 'Smelling out a Rat; – or the Atheistical-Revolutionist disturbed in his Midnight "Calculations"', 3 December 1790 — 26
4 James Gillray, 'Promis'd Horrors of the French Invasion, – or – Forcible Reasons for negociating a Regicide Peace', 20 October 1796 — 27
5 William Blake, 'The Ecchoing Green', from *Songs of Innocence and of Experience*, 1794, plate six — 29
6 William Blake, 'The Lamb', from *Songs of Innocence and of Experience*, 1794, plate eight — 29
7 George Cruikshank, 'Inconveniences of a Crowded Drawing Room', 1818 — 35
8 George Cruikshank, 'Massacre at St Peter's, or 'Britons Strike Home!!!', 1819 — 46
9 James Gillray, 'The New Morality', 1798 — 57

Preface

This book was first conceived in response to an invitation from the Open University to write the contextual units nine and ten for their course A362 'Romantic Poetry'. These units first appeared in 1984, and they have remained in use up to the present time. Over these five years I have received occasional comment on the units from students and tutors who had worked with them. Most of this comment has tended to suggest that the units to a large extent effectively served their purpose, of introduction to the main historical and social features of the Romantic period in England, and to the character of the literary culture in which Romantic poetry was first produced. But some comment also suggested limitations, particularly of sheer space in the treatment of such a large and complicated subject. It also became clear that the units might be of more general usefulness, to students in other forms of higher education and to the general reader, but that the special requirements of the Open University distance-learning format could be a distraction or even an obstacle for these readers. The present work is therefore offered as a considerably expanded and generally rewritten version of the original Open University units, intended for the use of general readers, or of undergraduate or advanced level students of the English Romantic poets who are coming to study of the writers and their contexts for the first time.

In addition to a virtual doubling of the text itself, I have added a literary and historical chronology of the period, and full bibliographies on the historical and literary context, and on each of the six major poets, Blake, Wordsworth, Coleridge, Byron, Shelley and Keats. There is also a somewhat different use of illustrations in the present book. The original units used illustrations to enliven the presentation and provide significant images of the period; here they are used more sparingly, and with a sharper attention to details of style and content, as these participate in important wider currents within the literary culture of the Romantics.

I am still indebted to the Open University course team who offered shrewd and tactful comments on the progress of the original units. I benefited in particular from the detailed advice of Angus Calder, Nick Furbank and, above all, Jokhim Meikle. Marilyn Butler, as external advisor to the team, was extremely helpful, and I should acknowledge here a general influence from Professor Butler's work which is evident in many pages of this book. I am also grateful to Rick Rylance and Alison Yarrington for their expert advice on various minute particulars. My expanded discussion of Byron's politics in this revised version partly draws on ideas exchanged with Drummond Bone and Len Findlay at a conference of the international Byron Society at the University of Groningen in Holland. The account of Shelley and science is a slightly revised version of part of an article first published in *Ideas and production*, 7 (1987). My thinking on some issues has been modified by rewarding conversation and correspondence with William Keach. Ray Cunningham, my literary editor at Open University Press, helped along the process of revision with patience and good humour. Finally, as ever, Faith Everest has been the most constructive and supportive of critical readers.

Introduction

The Romantic period in English literature may be considered as spanning roughly a 30-year period, from about the mid-1780s to the mid-1820s. British readers in this period considered their own contemporary literature as second only to that of Shakespeare in its quality and breadth, and this judgement has in subsequent years been repeatedly endorsed.

The Romantic movement falls into two generations or phases, although, as we shall see, these generations overlap and many features are continuous between them. The first generation included most importantly William Blake, William Wordsworth and Samuel Taylor Coleridge. The most important and influential writers of the second generation were Lord Byron, Percy Bysshe Shelley and John Keats. These were not necessarily the most fashionable or famous poets of their own times, nor were they the only poets to produce work of lasting value. At the beginning of the Romantic period English poetry was partly dominated by writers (such as, for example, Erasmus Darwin) who worked in a late Augustan tradition of rationally inclined couplet verse. Others, like William Cowper, cultivated a reflective, meditative poetry, often topographical, often rather melancholy, which has come to be thought of as 'pre-Romantic', and to be associated with the late eighteenth-century cultivation of sensibility. Later in the period the literary scene was often dominated by poets who continued to develop these traditions; Tom Moore, Thomas Campbell, Samuel Rogers and above all Sir Walter Scott, whose verse narratives were only displaced in popularity by the advent of Byron's successes as a narrative poet after 1812.

Other writers of the period worked at the margins of the literary culture, although they could exercise a charismatic influence upon it, as Robert Burns did. Some fine writers worked at the margins of polite society itself, although of the very many artisan poets of the early nineteenth century only John Clare – still an underrated and relatively neglected figure – overcame the formidable obstacles of his birth and education to produce poetry of a high order.

The six central Romantic poets nevertheless provide the main focus of this introduction to the poetry of the period. Their relation to the inherited literary tradition was the most innovative, the most conscious, and worked the most significant transformations within it. Their achievements also exerted by far the greatest influence on subsequent generations of British writers. Indeed, the Romantic influence is still very hard to disentangle from prevalent and widely shared assumptions about the very nature of poetry and the poet.

The six writers offer a rich diversity of achievement and preoccupation. This is not especially surprising. The movement of European culture known as Romanticism is chiefly remarkable for the range and variety of its forms; diversity itself is perhaps the most striking first impression made by Romantic art. The period which is dominated by our six writers displays the general sense of a newly exhilarating freedom from prescribed and agreed forms of expression, and from prescribed categories of perception and response. Blake and Wordsworth, for example, are each in their different ways profoundly original writers. Readers new to their work must immediately register the persisting strangeness of, for example, *The Marriage of Heaven and Hell* or the *Lyrical Ballads*. This strangeness is partly a matter of the difference between these books and what had gone before, and also partly a matter of the invention and creativity with which these writers co-ordinate heterogeneous stylistic and thematic materials. But the two books are also strikingly different *from each other*. The Romantic revolt is in a sense not so much a revolt against the shared standards and conventions of an earlier age; it is a revolt in a more thoroughgoing sense, against the very existence of dominating shared standards and conventions.

There are, however, clearly very important common interests and concerns which inform the work of the Romantic poets. Shared experiences, and a whole social world of inescapably given circumstances, contingencies and events, lie beyond the unique and distinctive qualities of each writer's work. It is particularly important to realize at once that this shared historical and social experience is not of a passive kind. Both generations of Romantic poets evince a profound engagement in the unfolding drama of their own times, and in this respect they are typical of a more general British cultural experience. For only very rarely has the larger movement of history impinged with such force on the private experience of individuals, as it did in the years from the outbreak of the French Revolution in 1789, to the great movement for political and social change that found one culmination in the 'Great Reform Bill' of 1832.

The objective of this book is to provide a perspective on the social and cultural milieu of the major romantic poets, for readers who are new to their work. Such readers will find it helpful to keep in mind that English society in the period from 1789 to 1832 was not static but constantly changing; changing on certain levels in a fundamental way. The England of the second generation of Romantics, Shelley, Keats and Byron, was not the England in which Blake, Wordsworth and Coleridge grew up and produced their earlier work. There was of course, though, a great deal that was continuous between the two periods, and it will be part of our concern to open up a view of the various continuities and differences between the social experience of the first- and second-generation Romantics. We shall attend to the broad sweep of social, political and cultural history as this bears upon the poets and their work; and we shall also attend to the more particular pressures that this complex historical development exerts on the specific forms and themes of Romantic poetry.

The discussion falls into three parts. The first part offers an outline of developments in the political, economic and social life of the nation, beginning in the years leading up to the French Revolution and ending in the third decade of the nineteenth century. This outline is further divided, in the interests of clarity, into three phases. The first phase begins with the aftermath of the American War of Independence (which began in 1775) and finishes in the period just before the outbreak of war between Britain and revolutionary France in 1793. The second phase covers the Anglo–French wars that continued, with two brief interruptions, from 1793 until the final defeat of Napoleon in 1815. The final phase comprises in conclusion the decade or so of social unrest and political confusion that followed the end of the war.

The second part of the discussion examines the social relations of the six major poets. By 'social relations' is meant the nature of their direct personal experience of the larger forces and events under consideration, and the bearing of this experience on their work as writers.

The third and final part surveys the more specifically literary milieu of the Romantic poets. Here attention is focused upon some interesting features of the poets' relations with the reviewers, and with the book trade and the publishers. This leads on to some general remarks about the role and social status of the poet in the early nineteenth century, and about the origins and possible significance of popular conceptions of literary Romanticism as these have developed during the Victorian age and on into our own time.

It may be helpful, though, to pause for a moment before approaching this range of contextual and historical material. It might reasonably be assumed that what this book offers is, in plain terms, a sketch of the 'background' to English poetry in the Romantic period. Indeed, it might well seem a natural assumption that the primary object of attention for a student of English literary Romanticism is a series of major works of literature. The rationale of any programme of study in a literary period would at least appear to be that great works of literature have their own irreducible value in virtue of aesthetic qualities which transcend the particular times and circumstances of their composition. These valued aesthetic qualities may indeed present themselves as more important, in the last analysis, even than the dominant thematic preoccupations of a particular poem. In other words, a poetic representation can for many serious readers be considered valuable not in its verisimilitude, or its power of instruction, but in its beauty. It is after all the case that out of all the thousands of poems written in England between 1789 and 1832, only a tiny proportion are now still read with pleasure and interest, and only a slightly larger proportion continue to be proposed for study on English literature courses in institutions of higher education.

Some of these unread poems are unjustly neglected, without a doubt. Other entire categories of poetry are marginalized and even suppressed by complex cultural mechanisms which have served vested social interests. The oblivion to which almost all Romantic poetry by women has been consigned is perhaps the most striking case in our present context. Much of this women's writing was impoverished and damagingly burdened from the start by the cultural disabilities imposed on women in their lack of education and generally subordinate social being. Subsequent neglect – almost no Romantic women's poetry is currently in print – has merely reinforced the original limitations of this mode of writing. Some poetry written by women in the Romantic period – by Charlotte Smith, Mrs Barbauld and Jane Taylor, for example – is undoubtedly worthy of serious attention by modern readers, and emphatically offers its own challenges and rewards. But the true context of this women's literature has still properly to be researched and understood, and must therefore fall outside the scope of the present study.

Nevertheless, it is clearly true to say that most of the poetry written in the Romantic period is relatively inept when judged by aesthetic criteria. And while it may prove true that some surviving poems – poems which still live in the consciousness of contemporary readers – originate in, and still refer us to, a very precise social or historical context, it is obvious that many poems no longer read have a social or historical reference which is equally direct, if not much more so. There is in other words a powerful sense in which the historical study of literature can seem an irrelevance, if a very absorbing one; it is simply that the social or historical reference of a poem is not what makes it good.

It is on the other hand evident that the understanding of poetry is greatly assisted by an awareness of its historical moment, and of its social origins. Poems are not conjured by their authors out of thin air; they are made out of history, and not just literary history, although that will obviously always be of the greatest importance amongst the many determinations that help to produce a work of literature. Wordsworth could not have written as he did if it had not been for James Thomson, for example, or William Cowper; none of these three could have written in blank verse as they did if it had not been for Milton. And for a second-generation Romantic such as Keats, both Milton and Wordsworth are inescapable and indispensable figures of the literary tradition that he inherited. In Shelley's mature work the presence of writers from diverse European traditions, the classical Greek dramatists, Rousseau, Dante, Petrarch, Calderon, is as inescapable and as formative as the most direct pressures of biographical time and place.

Literary history, however, is not in itself sufficient to account for the ways in which the Romantic poets modify and transform their inherited literary forms. For literary history belongs to a larger pattern of social change and development that is not the 'background' to literature, but is rather integral with it. Poets and poems are themselves part of history. Literature has a privileged but not qualitatively distinct position in the great complex of cultural, social and economic developments in which every writer's consciousness is caught up. The effort to give to poetry an alertly intelligent reading will necessarily involve the reader in an activity of historical judgement. Literary and historical judgements should then ideally enjoy a complementary and mutually substantiating relationship.

We are nevertheless still confronted with a problem when we consider literature in its social context. How are we to connect judgements of value in literary criticism with value-judgements in historical studies?

There are in the first instance two possible answers to this question. It may be decided at once that the question does not need to be asked: that literature is manifestly a world and a law unto itself, and that it exists in no necessary relation to history. But this view can only be sustained in intellectual comfort in the certainty that no social or historical judgements are, as it were, covertly present in the aesthetic effects that are valued.

The alternative is to seek for a rationally grounded method of integrating literary and historical judgement. It is only practicable in the present context to suggest some possible lines of thought that may be developed and modifed as the reader's own work and reflection on the Romantics' progresses.

The problem of how to integrate literary and historical judgement can be formulated for the purposes of argument by means of the concept of 'reference'. To what mental, or spiritual, or material phenomena is the reader directed or referred by the words that make up the literary work in question? Three alternative answers to this question may be proposed; self-reference, transcendent reference, or historical reference. Each alternative requires some brief explanation.

It is possible to understand literature as self-referring on the analogy of music. In this case, our attention is to an autonomous and unified work of art, self-sufficient, timeless and beautiful. It is made out of words, but the harmony of its internal relations of form is such that it escapes the social origins and reference of its words. Like a great piece of music, a great work of literature stands and is valued just in and for itself alone.

A second possible answer to the question of the reference of literature is the idea of 'transcendent reference'; by this is intended an approach to literature that finds it giving the reader access to permanent truths of human nature which transcend the particulars of time and place. These truths may be grounded in a highly worked-out philosophy, such as Christianity, or some form of Platonic Idealism. They may in contrast be understood as self-evident truths about 'Life', truths that every right-thinking and sensitive person already, intuitively as it were, possesses.

The third possible answer, 'historical reference', need not actually exclude our previous idea of transcendence. Literature can be understood to refer us to human experience as it takes an always particular form in the complex but motivated and causally coherent development of social reality. This line of thought may be developed in one of two ways.

The argument can be developed that history itself – the totality of human relations and institutions in their development through time – is the ultimately determining and defining reference of *all* human activity (including, for example, the perception of value and significance). A Marxist version of this historical approach to literary reference would take the further step of regarding history itself as motored by human economic development.

It is possible to reconcile this historical view, as indicated above, with the idea of transcendence. The development of history can be regarded as providing a material medium in which a higher purpose or design (perhaps divine) is worked out. As we shall shortly discover, this reconciliation of the historical and the divine was actually a prevalent view in the period of the first Romantics.

These general observations should hopefully assist towards a first consideration of some of the questions that are raised when literature is interpreted in its historical context. It is only sensible to bear in mind that such questions are always difficult, and are bound to seem baffling when they are broached for the first time.

PART ONE
The historical context

· ONE ·

Years of revolution: 1775–93

The outbreak of the French Revolution was registered in England with the dramatic news that the Bastille in Paris – a fortress prison that was the infamous symbol of despotic power – had been successfully stormed on 14 July 1789. Observers of every political colour recognized at once that here was an event of incalculable significance and implication. The specific range of English reaction will be considered shortly, but it will be helpful first to make some broad preliminary remarks about the circumstances that combined to give the Revolution its special significance for English people at that time.

The effect of the Revolution on English life was extraordinary. As one contemporary observer recalled, looking back across half a century, 'everything was connected with the Revolution in France, which for twenty years, was, or was made, all in all, everything; not this thing or that thing, but literally everything was soaked in this one event' (A. Cockburn, *Memorials of his Time*, 1856, p. 80). The impact of the Revolution owed its force to a convergence of four great orders of change: in politics (domestic and international), in the agrarian and the industrial economies, and in the population. These distinct but closely related orders of change were brought to focus in startling ways by the political ferment of the decade that followed the outbreak of the Revolution.

At the beginning of George III's reign in 1760 the population of England and Wales was probably rather less than seven million. By the time of the King's death in 1820 this approximate figure appears virtually to have doubled. While economists in the mid-eighteenth century argued fiercely about whether the population was growing, or static, or even decreasing, by 1798 the Tory intellectual Thomas Malthus could use a self-evident growth in the population to underpin the grim arguments of his *Essay on the Principle of Population*.

Both the causes and the effects of the increase in population are matters of great complexity and controversy. Certainly for our present purposes the change produced a new conception of the sheer extent and character of the English nation. This new conception was combined with the late eighteenth-century fact of literacy on a completely unprecedented scale; for the Romantic poets, a sense of the community to whom and for whom they spoke then assumes a novel importance. The problem of the audience for poetry comes to play a formative part in the Romantics' manner of address, and in the consciously 'democratic' cast of many of their themes and stylistic innovations.

The populousness of England at the turn of the century is inseparable from a decisive change in the nature of the economy. For this was also the period in which the country approached a spectacular take-off into self-sustaining economic growth. Here too questions of cause and effect are complex and controversial, but again certain effects exert a direct pressure on the experience and work of the Romantics.

The shift in economic emphasis from country to town, from agriculture to industry, was registered for contemporary English people as an increasingly marked transformation of the countryside and of urban life. It is impossible to overstress a simple and direct relationship in the period between the emergence of natural description in poetry in the English literary tradition (a development noticeable after 1700, then gathering momentum especially after the 1730s), and the influence of economic development on the actual appearance of rural England. Change in the agrarian economy was motored by a process of enclosure that had been under way since the time of Elizabeth. The altered face of English nature involved a loss of wild and common land, and an increasing preponderance of relatively undifferentiated large hedged fields. The eighteenth century saw great improvements in agricultural technology, and better machinery combined with the efficiency of enclosed fields to produce rural unemployment. As labour drifted towards new urban centres of industrial production, incipient rural depopulation and the consequent dilapidation of deserted dwellings became familiar facts of country life, and were treated as such by exponents and theorists of the rapidly expanding art and poetry of nature. The fashionable cult of the 'picturesque' flourished in these conditions, and found its text-books in the works of such men as William Gilpin. Gilpin's guide-books and accounts of tours, particularly in the Lake District in the later eighteenth century, brought a newly wild and abandoned character in the outposts of rural England into the orbit of polite taste, and effectively founded English tourism.

Conditions of work and life in the new urban industrial centres were much less quickly registered in the public mind; the shock of coming to terms with industrial England was essentially a Victorian experience. There were, though, some efforts to articulate an awareness of strange and wholly new social phenomena. The very early account by Robert Southey of industrial Birmingham at the beginning of the nineteenth century, included in his *Letters from England* of 1807, is a strikingly graphic example (Southey writes in the persona of a visiting Spanish nobleman):

> You will look perhaps with some eagerness for information concerning this famous city, which Burke, the great orator of the English, calls the grand toy-shop of Europe. Do not blame me if I disappoint you. I have seen much, and more than foreigners are usually admitted to see; but it has been too much to remember, or indeed to comprehend satisfactorily. I am still giddy, dizzied with the hammering of presses, the clatter of engines, and the whirling of wheels; my head aches with the multiplicity of infernal noises, and my eyes with the light of infernal fires, – I may add, my heart also, at the sight of so many human beings employed in infernal occupations, and looking as if they were never destined for anything better. Our earth was designed to be a seminary for young angels, but the devil has certainly fixed upon this spot for his own nursery-garden and hot-house . . . . When we look at gold, we do not think of the poor slaves who dug it from the caverns of the earth; but I shall never think of the wealth of England, without remembering that I have been in the mines . . . incredible as it may seem, a trifling addition to their weekly pay makes these short-sighted wretches contend for work, which they certainly know will in a very few years produce disease and death, or cripple them for the remainder of their existence.
>
> I cannot pretend to say, what is the consumption here of the two-legged beasts of labour; commerce sends in no returns of its killed and wounded. Neither can I say that the people look sickly, having seen no other complexion in the place than what is composed of oil and dust smoke-dried. Every man whom I meet stinks of train-oil and emery. Some I have seen with red eyes and green hair; the eyes affected by the fires to which they are exposed, and the hair turned green by the brass works. (Letter xxxvi)

Southey's account most powerfully conveys a sense of emphatically hellish disorientation ('giddy', 'dizzied'), and of moral revulsion at the nightmarish and unnatural human effects ('Some I have seen with red eyes and green hair') of a still-valued English commercial pride. The kind of social criticism implicit here is something to which we must return. In this context it signals a first consciousness of the deep changes in social relationships entailed by new modes of production. Only William Blake offers a sustained poetic response to these changes in the early Romantic period; the sadly oblivious or bitterly defiant voices of the child sweeps in *Songs of Innocence and of Experience* eerily prefigure great choruses of social protest yet to come. And Blake's 'satanic mills' figure also in the visual dimension of his illuminated prophecies, in a way which is, quite characteristically, many decades ahead of its time.

The French Revolution precipitated an intensity of political debate and popular initiative that exposed previously unsuspected fractures, contradictions and conflicts of interest in the social fabric of England. The first-generation Romantics grew to mature consciousness in this electrifying atmosphere of elation and crisis, and it is now appropriate to consider the specifically political forms in which this history was experienced in the last decade of the eighteenth century.

Coleridge suggested to Wordsworth in a letter of 1799 that he should shape his destiny as the great poet of his age by writing an epic account of the effects of the French Revolution on their own generation. The project grew in Wordsworth's mind, and he set out to work on 'The Recluse', as it came to be called. The autobiographical poem that was published after Wordsworth's death as *The Prelude* was originally conceived as the preliminary section of the greater work, and *The Excursion*, published in 1814, was a further instalment. In his Preface to the 1814 *Excursion* Wordsworth laid out his plan for the public, but it was never completed.

The original impulse and motive of the project, however, as proposed by Coleridge, remained firmly at the centre of those parts of 'The Recluse' that Wordsworth completed. The *Excursion* is concerned (at great length) with a representative post-Revolutionary despair and the means by which it might be 'corrected'. The poem's third book is entitled 'Despondency' and includes in its prefatory argument a sequence predicating the responses of the poem's central protagonist, 'The Solitary': 'His domestic felicity. – Afflictions. – Dejection. – Roused by the French Revolution. – Disappointment and disgust. – Voyage to America. – Disappointment and disgust pursue him. –' The following book is entitled 'Despondency Corrected', and avows the healing efficacy of 'belief in a superintending Providence' as the only enduring antidote to 'Disappointment from the French Revolution'. *The Prelude*, in each of its significantly distinct versions of 1799, 1805 and 1850, is also structured around the shock of the Revolution and Wordsworth's subsequent reactions to the course of events in France. In this emphasis on his experience of the French

Revolution, Wordsworth's is at once the most distinctive and the most characteristic poetic voice of the age. His initial elation, and his subsequent doubts and feelings of betrayal and despondency, were to lead finally to an embittered rejection of material social revolution as a false god; and this sequence constituted the typical intellectual biography of his contemporaries.

The successive phases of mood and event covered in Books Nine and Ten of the 1805 *Prelude* give in immensely illuminating detail the vivid extremes of response experienced by observers who shared Wordsworth's social and educational background in the early years of the Revolution. Wordsworth brilliantly shadows his evocation of the pristine elation and enthusiasm of those years with a saddened, elegiac tone, subtly endowed by the perspectives of a now older Englishman looking back in sober disenchantment on his earlier enthusiasm and gradual disillusionment:

> O pleasant exercise of hope and joy,
> For great were the auxiliars which then stood
> Upon our side, we who were strong in love.
> Bliss was it in that dawn to be alive,
> But to be young was very Heaven! O times,
> In which the meagre, stale, forbidding ways
> Of custom, law, and statute took at once
> The attraction of a country in romance –
> When Reason seemed the most to assert her rights
> When most intent on making of herself
> A prime enchanter to assist the work
> Which then was going forwards in her name.
> Not favoured spots alone, but the whole earth,
> The beauty wore of promise, that which sets
> (To take an image which was felt, no doubt,
> Among the bowers of Paradise itself)
> The budding rose above the rose full-blown.
> What temper at the prospect did not wake
> To happiness unthought of? The inert
> Were rouzed, and lively natures rapt away.
> They who had fed their childhood upon dreams –
> The playfellows of fancy, who had made
> All powers of swiftness, subtlety, and strength
> Their ministers, used to stir in lordly wise
> Among the grandest objects of the sense,
> And deal with whatsoever they found there
> As if they had within some lurking right

> To wield it – they too, who, of gentle mood,
> Had watched all gentle motions, and to these
> Had fitted their own thoughts (schemers more mild,
> And in the region of their peaceful selves),
> Did now find helpers to their hearts' desire
> And stuff at hand plastic as they could wish,
> Were called upon to exercise their skill
> Not in Utopia – subterraneous fields,
> Or some secreted island, heaven knows where –
> But in the very world which is the world
> Of all of us, the place in which, in the end,
> We find our happiness, or not at all.
>
> (Book Ten, ll. 689–727)

This account has come to be recognized as the quintessential articulation of English response in its decisive retrospective form; headiness pervaded by the sobriety of subsequent disillusion, the painful irony of that intransigent real world – 'the very world which is the world' – which was to prove such a hard place for happiness, after all.

Before we can understand, however, the extent and significance of English disillusion with the French example in the 1790s, it is essential to understand the force of the early idealizing acclaim and exultation in England in 1789, and to consider some of the reasons for this immediate enthusiasm.

Three lines of development contributed to an atmosphere in which the news of the Revolution was greeted, at first, by a great and extraordinary surge of joyous national optimism. These three established components of the national culture were a long native tradition of parliamentary democracy; a marked growth of political radicalism in the years following the American War of Independence; and the strong and articulate culture of English religious Nonconformity and Dissent.

There was indeed no reason for English people to be sorry that the nation's great economic and military rival appeared to have plunged itself into confusion; and there was, too, the gratification that France seemed to be discarding its monarchy in favour of English-style parliamentary government. England prided itself on the parliamentary democracy which had evolved since the 'Glorious Revolution' of 1688. With very little bloodshed this English 'Revolution' had effected the replacement of the extremely unpopular King James II, by the legal expedient of his abdication, with the succession of King William of Orange and his heirs. In fact a number of political clubs and societies had formed to celebrate the centenary of that Revolution in 1788, and they found splendid reason to meet again in the following year, to celebrate events in France. Almost all the opposition Whig politicians identified with the French cause (their party supported the liberties of the subject under the constitution, and fought the encroachments of royal patronage); the most eloquent parliamentary supporter of the French was the controversial and charismatic leader of the Whig party, Charles James Fox. But even the Tory Prime Minister, the younger William Pitt (he had been appointed to lead the government in 1783, aged just 24), found no real cause for alarm in the Revolution. It was, after all, a movement towards representative government, and England was the home of constitutionalism and representative institutions in eighteenth-century Europe; so, at least, her politicians liked to think.

Coleridge's very early poem 'Destruction of the Bastille' is representative of an enthusiastic but still politically moderate contemporary English response to the Revolution:

> Heard'st thou yon universal cry,
>   And dost thou linger still on Gallia's shore?
> Go, Tyranny! beneath some barbarous sky
>   Thy terrors lost and ruin'd power deplore!
>   What tho' through many a groaning age
>   Was felt thy keen suspicious rage,
>   Yet Freedom rous'd by fierce Disdain
>   Has wildly broke thy triple chain,
> And like the storm which Earth's deep entrails hide,
> At length has burst its way and spread the ruins wide . . .
>
> . . . Shall France alone a Despot spurn?
>   Shall she alone, O Freedom, boast thy care?
> Lo, round thy standard Belgia's heroes burn,
>   Tho' Power's blood-stain'd streamers fire the air,
>   And wider yet thy influence spread,
>   Nor e'er recline thy weary head,
>   Till every land from pole to pole
>   Shall boast one independent soul!
> And still, as erst, let favour'd Britain be
> First ever of the first and freest of the free!
>
> (ll. 1–10, 31–40)

This particular combination of political feelings – enthusiastic anticipation of an imminent international dimension to the revolutionary impulse, married with a serene confidence in 'favour'd Britain' as the very nursery of the ideals underlying the Revolution in France – was not to remain a sustainable or credible position for very long. But, for a short while in the early 1790s, it set the tone of response in a crucially formative way.

The loss of the American colonies in 1782 had been a disaster for George III and the government of the day. But once the political crisis had passed, the conflict proved to have repercussions far beyond the economic damage and the loss of diplomatic prestige that had seemed at the time most important. For the American war was observed and understood as a new kind of international conflict, involving primarily not issues of economic power, or of military competence, but fundamental principles of human rights. The American success inspired and nourished various British groups, some who were active in the campaign for suffrage and constituency reform in parliament, and others who laboured under the civil and religious disabilities that had passed into law since the break with Rome and the evolution of a politically wary Anglican Church. The agitation for parliamentary reform had grown since the 1770s, particularly in London, where it had focused on the contradictory personality of John Wilkes. By the late 1780s the reform movement was widely dispersed and oddly constituted; it lacked coherent structure, but was fortified by a spirit of rational enquiry and a readiness to engage what it saw as the small but powerful vested interests of the political status quo. These qualities were galvanized by the Revolution in France.

The reform movement received much of its energy, and most of its intellectual distinction, from the large, diverse community of Nonconformists and Dissenters. England was of course a Protestant country. The basic emphasis on individual responsibility which underlay the theology of the Reformation had long since led to further breaks, by groups of varying size, away from the episcopal structure of the Church of England. (The institution of bishops suggested externally imposed and state-sanctioned authority.) All such groups suffered the same kinds of legal disability as the Catholic community. Indeed their exclusion from the universities had produced a number of Dissenting 'Academies' of enviable intellectual quality (Oxford and Cambridge were generally unenlivened and educationally regressive during the period), and these institutions greatly enriched the cultural milieu of the Romantic generation.

One especially striking feature of the Dissenting enthusiasm for the Revolution was its metaphorical or even literal use of a millenarian perspective on political events. The Christian account of world history anticipated a second coming which would unite spiritual and political redemption. Biblical prophecy was considered by the more fervent and proselytizing sects to be approaching earthly realization in a miraculous transformation of political life, heralded in France and extending to all parts of human society. There was a largely working-class and artisan basis for the more extreme forms of millenial fervour (there was no shortage of candidates for the saviour himself). But even those highly educated intellectuals who professed the 'rational' persuasion of Unitarianism (denying the divinity of Christ, whom they thought of more as a kind of reformer) themselves used the language of Biblical prophecy, or at least of evangelical fervour, to set the tone of their political expectations in 1789 and 1790. The habit also carried over into the poetic practices of the first generation Romantics. Their frequent deployment of images of marriage, for example, often in very important poetic contexts, draws on the Biblical imagery of the millenium as a wedding (as found for instance in Revelation), and implicitly associates this imagery with the Romantic yearning for unity in the face of destructively fragmenting and socially alienating experience. The wedding party at the beginning and end of Coleridge's *Ancient Mariner* functions in this way, as does the familiar language of the 'Dejection Ode' which laments the passing of Coleridge's unifying poetic powers:

> O Lady! we receive but what we give,
> And in our life alone does nature live:
> Ours is her wedding-garment, ours her shroud!
>   And would we aught behold, of higher worth,
> Than that inanimate cold world allowed
> To the poor loveless ever-anxious crowd,
>   Ah! from the soul itself must issue forth
> A light, a glory, a fair luminous cloud
>   Enveloping the Earth –
> And from the soul itself must there be sent
>   A sweet and potent voice, of its own birth,
> Of all sweet sounds the life and element!
>
>   (ll. 47–58)

The very breadth and unity of English sympathy with the Revolution was its most remarkable feature; or so it appeared to radicals in the early years of the decade. The sense of joyous brotherhood made for a heady atmosphere. Possibilities were boundless; it seemed just a short step, and a generally desired one, to the material realization of a perfected society.

Public argument about the principles at stake in the Revolution began in earnest in 1790. The literature of political commitment and principle that this debate produced sets out the opposed positions of English politics in terms that have remained profoundly influential ever since. Above all, the conflict was perceived as being between the common people and a privileged and very wealthy social elite. (Whether this was *actually* the nature of the conflict is questionable.)

The debate was dominated by two men: Edmund Burke, the great

Whig statesman and parliamentary orator; and Thomas Paine, whose *Common Sense* (1776) had played a crucial part in the success of the American revolt. Burke's *Reflections on the Revolution in France* appeared in 1790 in response to a sermon, preached to a political club, that applauded the French Revolution. The preacher was Dr Richard Price, a leading Unitarian intellectual and radical sympathizer. Burke saw very early the full extent of what was at stake in the Revolution. His attack on it is a classic statement of the conservative outlook, and his defection to the Tories because of Whig support for the French sounded an early and ominous note of political reaction in England.

The *Reflections* associates revolutionary radicalism with a fanatical, pagan commitment to theory and abstraction that is criminally blind to the dictates of experience, tradition and the human wisdom accumulated by centuries of political practice and embodied in the Constitution. The book is a triumph of sustained rhetorical power. Burke's arguments for the monarchical status quo are chiefly backed up not by systematic reasoning but by a majestic, swelling tone of moral outrage and personal shock. It is its authenticity of personal emotion which gives the book its great power; together with Burke's organic view of the state, this makes the *Reflections* a recognizably Romantic work, even though its ideology is set defiantly against the revolutionary current in which the poets were to move.

The *Reflections* was enormously successful amongst the land-owning class whose interests it served. George III himself considered the work compulsory reading for every gentleman in the land. Burke's book also called forth numerous replies from the radicals (the pre-Romantic poet William Cowper complained that he could not find a printer to produce his translation of Homer because all the presses were busy with replies to Burke). Far and away the most important of the replies was by Burke's former friend Tom Paine. His *Rights of Man* (published in 1791 and supplemented in 1792 by a second part) countered the consciously subjective and emotional manner of the *Reflections* with a plain, forthright and rational style that itself made a basic democratic point. The style scorned finery, and opened the field of debate to all men, of whatever education or class; with the *Rights of Man*, the English language became *generally* available as a tool of persuasion and propaganda. Its sales tapped the resources of a newly literate population, and seemed to contemporaries to indicate an audience of a size which was scarcely credible. Over the first decade after its publication, sales of Paine's book were reckoned (admittedly by Paine himself) in millions. From the point of view of the authorities it was far more serious that such a vast readership should exist at all, than that it had access to any actual ideas. The specific content of Paine's politics was not in fact so very revolutionary; his views have even been construed as amounting to an advocacy of free-market capitalism that was not fundamentally at odds with the interests which Burke sought to defend. It was Paine's tone that was his most subversive feature, just as it was in the writings of other discursive political commentators of the period – journalists such as William Cobbett, for example – who reached similarly vast audiences, and who sharply focused and brought to telling articulation a whole range of popular social and cultural discontents. Paine provided an inspirational rallying-point for the emergent working-class radicalism of the 1790s, that was to grow eventually into the Trade Union and Labour movements of our own time. His work thereby proved far more durable than the other efforts of response to Burke, by radicals whose social interests were different, and who suffered irrecoverably from the dark years of political reaction and repression soon to come.

Two other replies to Burke deserve brief notice for their bearing on the work of the Romantic poets, though neither work offered itself as a direct response to the *Reflections*. They were, however, very much the products of the climate of intense radical speculation that was stimulated by Burke's book. William Godwin's *Enquiry Concerning Political Justice* appeared in 1793; Mary Wollstonecraft's *Vindication of the Rights of Women* was published in 1792.

Godwin was a radical atheist from a Dissenting background (his family were Sandemanians). *Political Justice* offered a somewhat self-consciously abstract outline of 'philosophical anarchy', which objected to all constraints whatsoever on the operation of pure reason (constraints such as governments, family, emotions). In a famous example Godwin insisted that, confronted with a situation where it was possible to save from death by fire either a respected philosopher, or one's own wife or mother, reason would dictate that the philosopher be saved, because that course of action would yield the most benefit to people in general. Godwin's work was the most influential book of the 1790s amongst the Dissenting radical-intellectual community, which included Blake, Wordsworth and Coleridge (though Coleridge's Christianity made him a critic of Godwin), and also such now less well-remembered intellectuals and agitators as the dramatist Thomas Holcroft and the radical lecturer John Thelwall.

It is interesting to note the extremely confined audience for Godwin's political writing. As the atmosphere in England changed, so Godwin's celebrity faded (in contrast to Paine's), and this fact points most significantly to the absence of any popular basis for Godwin's circle of (mostly) London radical intellectuals and their ideas. This had consequences that must be pursued in the next section of our discussion.

Mary Wollstonecraft was a courageous and adventurously independent woman who experienced some notoriety (and much suffering too) by the conduct of her private life. She was for a short time married to

Plate 1 William Blake, *Visions of the Daughters of Albion*, 1793, frontispiece

Godwin before her death after childbirth in 1797 (the baby grew up to become Shelley's second wife Mary, the author of *Frankenstein*). Her *Vindication* is interesting today as much for its contradictions (an unwillingness or inability to cast her attack on male dominance in adequately radical terms) as for its rationalist stress on education. Amongst her contemporaries, her feminism, for all its uncertainty and carefully respectful manner, met with almost universal contempt and derision. But there is good reason to mention *Vindication* (apart from its quite recent retrieval by the present-day feminist movement): her work has an important bearing on two of the Romantic poets. Blake knew Mary Wollstonecraft well (it seems), and he developed her views on the subjection of women in his own brilliant and strangely original illuminated poems about female consciousness and sexuality, *The Book of Thel* (1789), *Europe* (1794), and, above all, *Visions of the Daughters of Albion* (1793) (Plate 1). *Visions* is an extraordinary production for its time, drawing on Wollstonecraft's parallels between the condition of women and the condition of slaves to create a powerfully critical representation of the contradictions and destructive force of male sexual jealousy and violence. Blake's 'prophecy' offers a vision of women's socio-sexual dilemma in terms which integrate it with other corruptions of human potentiality, in the economic arena – England was at the centre of the world slave trade – and in the international dimension of Britain's position as an incresingly confident and aggressive imperial power. This range takes him beyond Wollstonecraft's perspectives, but she was a crucial part of the intellectual matrix which made Blake's art possible.

Shelley was the other poet to utilize Wollstonecraft's ideas on the need for female equality, and on the political dimension of male dominance. He came under her influence particularly after his elopement with her daughter Mary in 1814 (something which proved too testing for Godwin's rationalism) and he seems to have known the whole range of Wollstonecraft's published writings in close detail. The influence is most emphatic in the long and daring revolutionary poem of 1817, *Laon and Cythna* (more widely known in its revised version as *The Revolt of Islam*), which is now neglected and underrated. But Wollstonecraft's imprint may also be discerned in the visions of sexual relations in a post-revolutionary society which come towards the end of the third act of Shelley's finest poem, *Prometheus Unbound*.

· TWO ·
Years of reaction:
1793–1815

The initial optimism that welcomed news of the French Revolution soon collapsed with an embittering and intensely disheartening completeness. As events in France took their course, they fuelled a developing reactionary and nationalist tendency in English life. For the radicals, the collapse of confidence in the possibility of social change for the better, coming so rapidly after the early excitement, was an absolutely shattering experience. It has been powerfully argued that this experience was one of the fundamental determinants of a subsequent Romantic commitment to the imagination and the inner resources of the self. Influential critics such as the American M. H. Abrams have sought to show that the mind and heart were territories in which the disappointed radical could shelter and resurrect broken ideals, on a strictly personal and domestic level. It is however advisable to bear in mind that critical judgements have their own historical context. The views of Abrams, and of other American critics who stress a quasi-mystical element and example in this version of the Romantic experience, may be reading something of their own experience and background into their formulations of the Romantic ethos, and of what they take to be its characterstic forms and preoccupations. It is, on the other hand, equally possible to argue that there was a newly charged political dimension in the Romantic representation of private consciousness.

The major European states soon realized that the French Revolution represented a challenge to the very basis on which they were constituted. From the early 1790s Great Britain, Austria, Prussia, and a varying range of other European powers formed shifting 'defensive' alliances against the Revolutionary government. Their diplomatic and military initiatives were justified by growing evidence of internationalist zeal on the part of the French. The Revolution, it seemed, was to be carried to the peoples of Europe.

Fox, leader of the parliamentary Whigs, was discredited by sustaining his support for the Revolution after the tide of ruling-class opinion had decisively turned. As more and more prominent opposition politicians joined the Tories, Pitt supervised a strategy by which the Whigs were manoeuvred into political impotence. For a quarter of a century there was no effective challenge to the government within the conventional order of British politics. This enabled Pitt's ministry to carry out an effective campaign of repression against dissident elements, especially after war had officially broken out between England and France in February 1793. After that, support for the French was not only unpopular; it was treason.

The government promoted a crudely derogatory image of the French revolutionaries and their British supporters, to complement its legal measures against assemblies and combinations. The propaganda found its most potent form, as the decade went on, in the enormously popular political cartoons of James Gillray, whose pro-government work thereby reached an audience far greater than anything produced by the radicals. It was a bitter irony that the cause of the people became in the 1790s an object of hostility, not least from the majority of the common people. By the mid 1790s public opinion had swung solidly behind the government in a loyalist reaction to the war itself.

It can, however, be misleading to read the cultural products of the time in a way which finds them comfortably in harmony with a larger reading of history. Certainly, Gillray's prints functioned in the way characterised above as 'pro-government'. They do, however, present in themselves a more complex case than at first seems apparent. It is instructive to attend briefly to the nature of this complexity, for it points to a more generic feature of Romantic art and writing in the period of the French wars.

Gillray's prints which represent directly the violent events in France are indeed unequivocal in their savage condemnation. 'The Zenith of French Glory: The Pinnacle of Liberty', for example (Plate 2), which is dated 12 February 1793, is a plain and unironized depiction of the guillotine (and indeed a literally accurate one; Gillray had a good nose for what the public might like to see). Its imminent use – the King's head is about to be cut off – is gawped at by a large crowd, uniformly sporting the 'bonnet rouge', complete with cockade, which was the acknowledged mark of the revolutionary supporter. The ruffianly revolutionary figured in the foreground fiddles while the grand ecclesiastical building in the background burns down. Priests and monks swing from the lamp-holder, as does a judge, together with the emblems of justice, from the one beneath the central figure. In a very characteristic verbal-visual pun, the

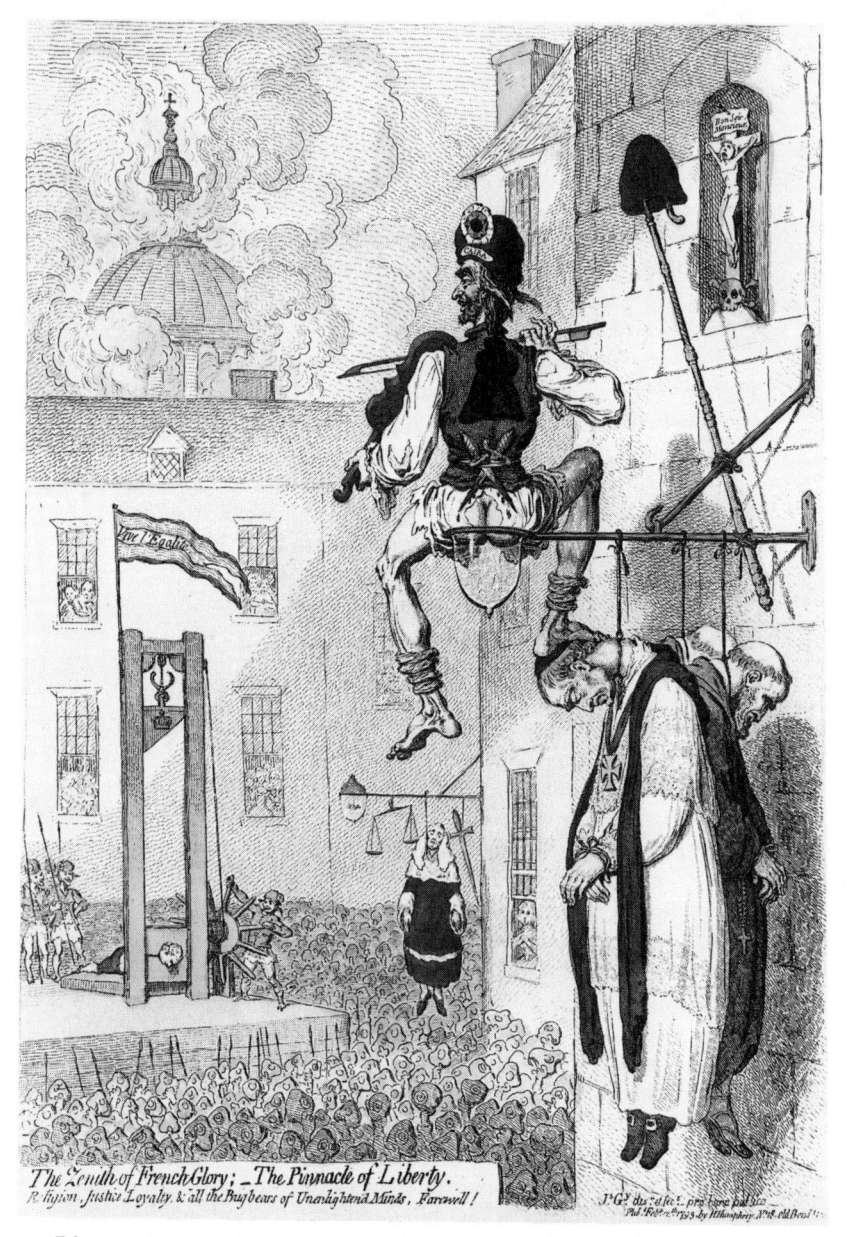

Plate 2 James Gillray, 'The Zenith of French glory; – The Pinnacle of Liberty. Religion, Justice, Loyalty, & all the Bugbears of Unenlightened Minds, Farewell!', 12 February 1793

'sans-culotte' presents a mildly obscene image, perhaps suggesting the approach of a moral defecation. The tone of the print is angrily condemnatory.

But Gillray's images of English response to events in France are in fact far more ambivalent than this, and often escape any easy political affiliation by their baffling reserve and contrariety of implication. Even such a familiar and apparently obvious print as 'Smelling out a Rat; – or the Atheistical-Revolutionist disturbed in his Midnight "Calculations"', dated 3 December 1790 (Plate 3), is not quite targeted in the way that is often assumed. An extravagantly snooping Burke – cleverly adapting the caricaturist's received image of the physiognomic detail – swoops down in a cloud on the surprised Dr Price. He is represented as perfectly normal, if foolish (mainly in virtue of the representative texts around him, and the image of Charles II's execution on the wall behind him). The implication is that he pursues his pseudo-scientific radical 'Calculations' without working out in advance where they might lead. But Burke is unmistakably the physically derided figure, and his portentous bearing of the emblems of Church and state hints at a possible self-interested motive in his abandonment of the Whigs in favour of an arch Tory rhetoric and position (and indeed a government pension, as his radical opponents never tired of noticing).

In short, the print caricatures Burke's reaction to Price's sermon which prompted the *Reflections on the Revolution in France*, every bit as much as it caricatures Price himself. This unexpected doubleness of perspective is very often present in Gillray's work of the 1790s on English subjects. It is a stylistic feature perhaps best understood in relation to various cognate instances in the Romantic period of an art founded on unresolved conflicts, or which reaches towards a formal expression of dialectic which never arrives at synthesis. One of the most striking of all instances of this formal quality in Gillray's oeuvre is the complex and very diverting 'Promis'd Horrors of the French Invasion, – or – Forcible Reasons for negociating a Regicide Peace', dated 20 October 1796 (Plate 4) and evidently prompted initially by Burke's majestically alarmist pamphlet *Letters on a Regicide Peace*, which appeared in the same year. The image teems with recognizable figures from contemporary party politics, in the setting of a St James's Street (the Tory's club, White's, is on one side of the road; the Whig club, Brooks's, on the other) down which marches a huge and monstrous French revolutionary army. Whig politicians collaborate furiously and fiendishly with the enemy – the detail is extraordinarily rich and inventive – and the whole range of Tory parliamentarians and supporters meet diversely grisly deaths or torture. The print cannot plausibly be read as an appalled cautionary image of what might actually happen in the event of an invasion. Pious horror is

Plate 3 James Gillray, 'Smelling out a Rat; — or the Atheistical-Revolutionist disturbed in his Midnight "Calculations"', 3 December 1790

Plate 4 James Gillray, Promis'd Horrors of the French Invasion, – or – Forcible Reasons for negociating a Regicide Peace', 20 October 1796

too relentlessly and amusingly fused with ludicrous images of establishment figures. The overall effect is rather that of a laughable representation of exaggerated and completely implausible fears on the part of the status quo. The true target is not revolutionary France, but the establishment England which manipulated wartime anxieties to stage a massive consolidation of its hold on power in the public imagination.

Gillray's unresolved ambivalence enables his art to register the deep disjunctions and conflicts in the social fabric, without declaring absolute commitment at the level of political interest. Other, even greater Romantic artists achieve a comparable elusive balance in their artistic responses to the same conflicts and divisions. Blake's *Songs of Innocence and of Experience* (1789–94) embody a formal organization of constantly self-qualifying and mutually modifying elements, working on several different levels at once. The meaning, for example, of the plate on which the first part of the 'Innocence' poem 'The Ecchoing Green' appears (Plate 5), is partly constituted by the words on the page, so to speak. But these words are modified by their participation in relationships, on similar and on different levels, which are comprised in the larger series of the entire sequence of poems in the collection. Lyric poems spoken in the voices of children can, for instance, in other poems in the series, suggest an ignorance of real social conditions (think of 'The Chimney Sweeper' poem in *Innocence*) which limits and ironizes the child's simple sincerity and joy. The knowledge of this possible perspective modifies our reading of similar perspectives elsewhere, as in the text of 'The Ecchoing Green'. But this text is modified as well by its perplexing relation to the image which accompanies it (the old folks are *not* laughing away care), and this image is modified in its turn by its implicit juxtaposition with similar images in other plates in the work (for example the sheltering tree echoes differently contextualized instances on the *Innocence* title page, and in the design accompanying 'The Lamb' (Plate 6)). Indeed each and every one of the plates in *Blake's Songs* has a complex meaning which inheres in – and in practice constantly disappears into – the multiple networks of relationship in which each engraved plate is caught up.

Even a writer like Jane Austen, who is in many ways in an entirely oppositional and antagonistic overt relation to the characterizing formal qualities of Romantic art, displays a kind of affinity with the unresolved dialectic of Blake and Gillray. Her subtle fictional endorsements of the landed ruling order in English life dramatize the saving survival under threat of a highly privileged social class. Dangerous tendencies to socially destructive modes of self-fulfilment, and to disordering self-interested modifications of the social order, are placed and thwarted by the delicate logic of plot. Nevertheless, certain socially unaccommodated human impulses and potentialities do survive their defeat at the level of the action

Plate 5 William Blake, 'The Ecchoing Green', from *Songs of Innocence and of Experience*, 1794, plate six

Plate 6 William Blake, 'The Lamb', from *Songs of Innocence and of Experience*, 1794, plate eight

in the novels. Mr Bennett is sternly rebuked by the turn of events in *Pride and Prejudice*, but his devastating personal judgements express a liberatingly anarchic version of his social world which enters a fundamental question about the extent to which the values of that world are ratified by the implicit judgements of the novel. A somewhat similar unresolved doubleness of perspective is present in the treatment of Elizabeth Bennett herself. And there are equally perplexing ambivalences of this kind in, for example, the nearly fatal tribulations of Marianne Dashwood in *Sense and Sensibility*, or in the curious moral waverings which dog Fanny Price at crucial moments in her path to a comfortable eminence in the re-established order of *Mansfield Park*.

It is then not at all surprising that Romantic poetry, the art form in which generic features of Romanticism are most consciously and influentially present, should ubiquitously display varieties of formal innovation which articulate the experience of a social world in deep and uncertainly directed conflict.

The course of events in France was followed closely throughout the early 1790s, and with mounting alarm, by English people. The occupation of the Tuileries Palace in August 1792, leaving some 1,200 dead, was rapidly followed by suspension of the monarchy and the introduction of universal male suffrage. In September, in the embattled confusion of panic over a threatened invasion by Prussia, there was an appalling slaughter of 'enemies of the Revolution'. Louis XVI was executed in January 1793, and aggressive French intentions towards Holland, and the vital trade route of the Scheldt river, became unmistakable. England had a reciprocal defence treaty with Holland, and war followed automatically. A bloody counter-revolutionary uprising in the Vendée was fought out from March right through to the end of 1793. On 16 October the execution of Marie-Antoinette appeared dreadfully to confirm Burke's tragic vision of the French Queen that had formed the rhetorical centre of his *Reflections*. The 'Girondins', the group who had been responsible for the radicalization of the revolution, were themselves overthrown and executed towards the end of 1793 by the more extreme 'Jacobins' under Robespierre ('Jacobin' also became at this time an abusive word for an English radical). Robespierre's notorious butchery in the 'terrors' of 1793–4, followed by still more killings and changes of leadership and direction in France, had by the mid-1790s left the hopes of sympathetic British observers in irretrievable ruin.

The bloody failure of the Revolution is referred to in Act I of Shelley's lyrical drama *Prometheus Unbound*. Two semichoruses of 'Furies' – who here represent reactionary forces which welcomed the disillusioning carnage – taunt the suffering hero with emblems of the failure of human idealism and hope. Their speeches vividly evoke the sickening prospect which confronted those English radicals who had looked to France for their inspiration:

Semichorus I

> See, a disenchanted Nation
> Springs like day from desolation;
> To Truth its state is dedicate,
> And Freedom leads it forth, her mate;
> A legioned band of linkèd brothers
> Whom Love calls children –

Semichorus II

> 'Tis another's –
> See how kindred murder kin!
> 'Tis the vintage-time for Death and Sin:
> Blood, like new wine, bubbles within;
>   Till Despair smothers
> The struggling World – which slaves and tyrants win.
>   (Act I, ll. 564–77)

It is of the first importance to grasp the direct bearing of the English response to these events on the lives of radical-intellectual French sympathizers such as Blake, Wordsworth and Coleridge. They faced not only bitter disillusion but also acute social discomfort. Their egalitarian opinions earned them extreme and open hostility. And this hostility came, as we shall see later, not only from the typically loyal, God-fearing Englishman who lived in the village; it came too, in a perhaps less escapable form, from the great majority of that educated gentry class who constituted (certainly for Wordsworth and Coleridge) the social peers of the Romantics.

The most essential thing, however, to bear in mind about this period of the 1790s, is the pervasive character of the social and political crisis. Every sphere of life was affected, everybody had their opinions and actively engaged convictions. Ideas that can seem to us now remote from political implication had at the time dramatic force as extensions of the radical democratic position. Matters of poetic style, for example, and, no less important, of literary theory, took their resonance and their implicit polemical alignment from within the oppositions of political belief that raged throughout those years.

The wars with France lasted longer than anyone at the start had imagined they would. The military career of Napoleon gradually brought him to prominence and power in the 1790s, and he assumed absolute power as First Consul under the new French constitution of November 1799. In Napoleon, France had a leader with the extraordinary abilities, and the driving political will, to launch the nation on a crusading campaign to unite Europe under a single Emperor. The Napoleonic wars consequently involved almost the whole of Europe. Apart from one brief respite of some 14 months after the Peace of Amiens in March 1814 (and one other brief period of a few months at the end of 1814), England was at war with France from February 1793 until the end of the 'hundred days' – the period between Napoleon's escape from his first exile on Elba, and his final defeat at Waterloo – in June 1815.

These wars were of a new kind. War had customarily been an affair of small professional armies, often mercenaries, and its effects on everyday life had been for the most part relatively slight. But France in the 1790s had mobilized as a nation in the face of what appeared the hostility of the whole continent, and the strain on England's economy, and on her executive and military structure, was enormous. Life in England evolved a defensive cultural insularity that severely hampered every kind of French influence, including the translation of books. Germany, on the other hand, made up of quite small territories that were vulnerable to French imperialism, was pro-English, and its literature and philosophy began (after the turn of the century) to enter gradually but powerfully into English cultural life.

The war did not go well for England for some years. Not until the campaign in Spain and Portugal that began in 1807 did Napoleon's resources begin to appear seriously stretched. An atmosphere of backs-to-the-wall resistance in England generated intense nationalist fervour. This was memorably focused on such war heroes as Lord Nelson, whose death in the naval victory at Trafalgar in 1805 occasioned a spectacular outburst of national mourning and determined solidarity.

By the late 1790s much radical support had been dissipated by the sweep of events, or had gone underground in the face of government persecution. This persecution was mainly exercised by the manipulation of mob violence, and by the operation of a large and notorious domestic spy system. Blake, Wordsworth and Coleridge suffered from this government campaign in immediate and personal ways, and they fought throughout most of the 1790s to preserve their radical integrity and independence. But the social and psychological pressure of a fiercely combative national cultural identity told in its effects on the poets. Most of the radicals of the earlier 1790s had, by the second decade of the new century, been borne along with the current of the times into a conservative orthodoxy. It was in this guise that they confronted a new generation which was becoming articulate towards the end of the war.

Byron had been born in the year before the Revolution, Keats and Shelley in the early 1790s. As the war drew to a close the disillusioned generation of the revolutionary decade came to be seen by these young radicals as the apostate servants of a contemptible orthodoxy in politics and religion.

The major literary productions of the last war years, Wordsworth's *Excursion* and Jane Austen's *Mansfield Park* (both published in 1814), are monuments of English cultural insularity in its period of deepest and most self-confident reactionary feeling. Wordsworth in particular – whose earlier poetry and poetic theories were so deeply influential on the new young poets – appeared a despicable figure in his ponderous lauding of Anglican theology and the status quo. Indeed, wherever the second-generation Romantics looked they found corruption and killing intellectual stagnation in their native country. This ethos was personified in the grossly fat and grotesquely vain and egocentric figure of the Prince Regent. He had ruled since 1812 in place of his father, who was overwhelmed in that year by an illness whose symptoms closely resembled insanity. Shelley evokes these rulers, and the cultural atmosphere of the Regency as it was experienced by the young radical poets, in his fine sonnet 'England in 1819'. The poem evokes with brilliant economy the social and cultural ethos that was to drive Shelley and Byron into exile, and that contributed to Keat's tragically early and embittered death:

> An old, mad, blind, despised and dying King;
> Princes, the dregs of their dull race, who flow
> Through public scorn, – mud from a muddy spring;
> Rulers who neither see nor feel nor know,
> But leechlike to their fainting Country cling
> Till they drop, blind in blood, without a blow;
> A people starved and stabbed on the untilled field;
> An army whom liberticide and prey
> Makes as a two-edged sword to all who wield;
> Golden and sanguine laws which tempt and slay;
> Religion Christless, Godless, a book sealed;
> A senate, Time's worst statute, unrepealed,
> Are graves from which a glorious Phantom may
> Burst, to illumine our tempestuous day.

For all the anger and social commitment here, however, there is a sceptical reserve implicit in the shaping of this poem. This again suggests that characteristic Romantic ambivalence which we have already noted in relation to such artists as Blake, Gillray and Austen. The sonnet – prompted by news of the Peterloo massacre of 1819, which we shall come to in the next chapter – lists a whole series of social and political evils which are ironically positive in their long-term effects because they will help to create the conditions for a transforming social revolution. And yet, the placing of the auxilary verb 'may' in the penultimate line throws the emphasis onto a conditional and hesitant tone which modifies the force of the poem's overt political sentiment. This ironizing reserve, or drawing back from an unqualified assent to absolute statements, is very characteristic of basic formal features in Romantic poetry.

The national identity that was forged by the years of struggle against Napoleonic France was complex and contradictory, like the cultural forms which it helped to produce, and which in turn shaped that identity. The components of this national identity are brilliantly specified, and arranged as attributes of various representative public figures, in William Hazlitt's *The Spirit of the Age* (1825). This work offers a particularly valuable and interesting perspective on its own times, because its structural principle, whereby personalities are represented as caught inescapably in the complex cross-currents of their culture, constitutes the perfect model for the social experience of the Romantic intellectual. Progressive and reactionary elements of the national culture tended to blur party oppositions. The last excesses of Regency high life – the London of Beau Brummel and the Dandies, of the Hellfire Club and the compulsive drinking, gambling and whoring of ne'er-do-well eldest sons – existed side by side with a new seriousness and 'respectability' in middle-class norms of behaviour. It has been remarked that Englishmen of the Napoleonic and post-war years were 'the fathers of the Victorians', and it is helpful to consider some manifestations of incipient 'Victorianism' in English life. This will provide a sense of context for the attitudes adopted by the second-generation Romantic poets who produced their work between 1812 and the mid-1820s.

Three features of the national culture in early nineteenth-century England are particularly pertinent: the rise of Evangelicalism in religion; new developments in the traditionally British academic discipline of 'political economy'; and a growing awareness of change in the quality of working life, rural and urban, that began to give serious cause for alarm.

The Anglican Church had towards the end of the eighteenth century fallen into what seems now a lamentable state of apathy and complacently corrupt practices, of which the most familiar (in Jane Austen's novels, for example) was clerical absenteeism. The Methodist movement, inspired by John Wesley, had breathed new life into English religious experience, and not simply into the Anglican establishment: but Dissenting sects, which flourished in circumstances of persecution, had also rather mellowed (from their more typical enthusiasm and fervour) in the lax atmosphere of non-enforcement of repressive legislation.

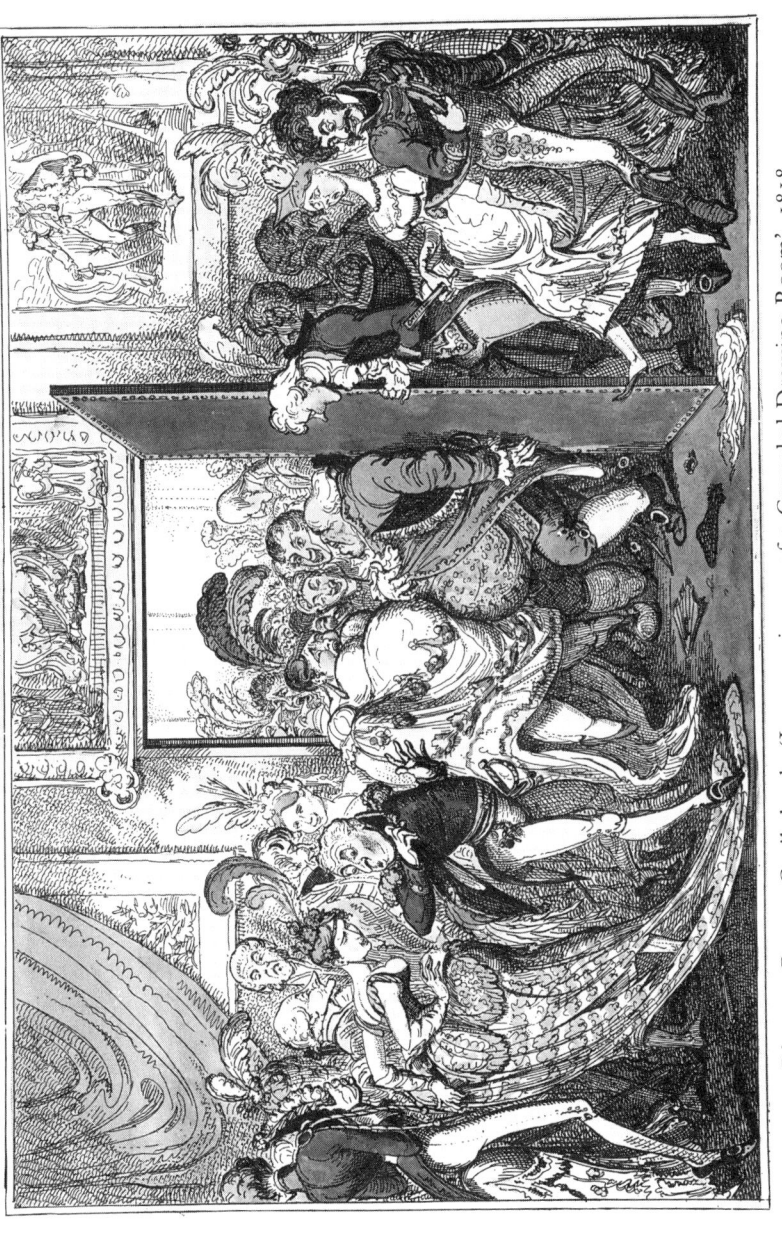

Plate 7 George Cruikshank, 'Inconveniences of a Crowded Drawing Room', 1818

A new spirit of energetic public engagement by committed Christians was abroad in the late 1780s and 1790s, amongst the Dissenters certainly, but also amongst certain 'Evangelical' Anglicans whose social background gave them scope for activity in affairs of public life, and in 'Society' itself. The best known of the Evangelicals were Hannah More and William Wilberforce (Wilberforce was a leading member of the famous 'Clapham Sect').

In the 1780s Hannah More had supplemented Wesley's work amongst the great mass of the people by addressing herself to the raising of moral consciousness in polite society. Her work was highly successful (if book sales are a guide), and in the 1790s she extended her activities to countering 'ungoldly' Painite propaganda on behalf of that same polite society over whose behaviour she had kept a watchful eye. Wilberforce similarly exemplifies the Evangelical commitment to active Christian intervention in public life. He most notably led the campaign against slavery (primarily a British industry in the early nineteenth century), and generally contributed to a heightened sense of moral duty and responsibility in the war years. The positive form of this new 'respectability' in public and domestic affairs was a genuine concern for 'the poor' and for issues of social distress and public malpractice. But its negative form was a hardening of national insularity and a growing mistrust of all things 'continental', combined with the evolution of an impenetrably self-righteous and straight-laced rectitude in family life. An economically ascendant middle class was happy to find in its own blinkered and bigoted values a repository of timeless virtues. These recognizably Victorian qualities (the classic 'bourgeois' values) are formed in the Romantic period, and they have a crucial effect too on the way in which Romantic poetry itself comes to be regarded, throughout the nineteenth century and into our own times.

Victorian values were also emerging in the more technical field of economic theory, which had found a natural home in Britain with the remarkable expansion of industry and commerce. Here a quasi-scientific rationalization of the values of industrial and mercantile capitalism was presented as an account of natural laws at work within the economy. Old-fashioned paternalism in industrial relations was argued away in theory (as it had vanished in fact) to clear the road for an 'objective' recognition of market forces. This 'political economy', elaborated chiefly by David Ricardo (who was building on foundations laid in the previous century by Adam Smith), was in practice equally available, essentially as a justification of *laissez-faire* policies, to both progressive and reactionary positions. This disconcerting interchange of arguments and attitudes between opposed political interests then emerges yet again as an especially interesting feature of the Romantic period. It also testifies to a general breakdown, at the end of the continental wars, of the established divisions of the political order.

The value of science was one striking instance of this ambivalence. The political economists were in one sense the heirs of Bentham. His doctrine of 'Utilitarianism', which set as the goal of human choice and action 'the greatest happiness of the greatest number', was appropriated to serve humanitarian initiatives. But it was also used to justify the most brutally rationalist 'general good' arguments and policies that paid no heed to the reality of the particular human ills which might result. Scientific rationalism could thus be seen as the saviour of man, but also as the theoretical basis of capitalist arguments for efficiency and the maximization of profit as absolute goods, irrespective of any human cost.

The resulting association of science with a humanly destructive industrial capitalism is a very important component of the thought of the Romantic poets. Blake's general rejection of science and empirically based reasoning comes remarkably early. He perceived the implications of a dominance of scientific over imaginative modes of thought almost before the conflict had taken material form in English culture. Blake therefore threw his own weight as an artist on the side of the irrational and the imaginative; not because he was a mystic, but because of the exigencies of his social–historical analysis. More influentially at the time, Wordsworth displayed a confident anti-rationalism – 'we murder to dissect' – which became widely current through the arguments of the Preface to *Lyrical Ballads*. An extremely influential formulation in the 1800 Preface opposes poetry to science: 'much confusion has been introduced into criticism by [the] contradistinction of poetry and prose, instead of the more philosophical one of Poetry and Matter of Fact, or Science.'

Here the real opposition is of science – 'Matter of Fact' – to imagination, the unifying and creative power of mind from which in the Romantic view derives all meaning and value in experience. It is the opposition which underlies Coleridge's still more influential formulation of 'Imagination and Fancy' (most famously in the thirteenth chapter of his *Biographia Literaria* (1817)); Coleridge characterized the Fancy as a mental faculty having 'no other counters to play with, but fixities and definites.' The world of the scientist's perception is dead, inorganic, discrete.

The attack on science in Keats's *Lamia* (1820) is also pertinent in this context:

> Do not all charms fly
> At the mere touch of cold philosophy?
> There was an awful rainbow once in heaven:

> We know her woof, her texture; she is given
> In the dull catalogue of common things.
> Philosophy will clip an Angel's wings,
> Conquer all mysteries by rule and line,
> Empty the haunted air and gnomèd mine –
> Unweave a rainbow, as it erewhile made
> The tender-personed Lamia melt into a shade.
>
> (Part II, ll. 229–38)

By 'philosophy' here Keats means what was then known as 'natural philosophy', i.e. science. The true target in these lines is Newton, whose analysis of the spectrum is deemed to have destroyed the mysterious splendour of a miracle of nature, just as the cold philosopher (and academic) Apollonius destroys the beautiful and – by this stage in the poem – sympathetic and vulnerable character of Lamia. It is, though, wise to be cautious, here as elsewhere in Romantic poetry, in assigning a too schematic interpretation to the passage and its function within the poem as a whole. The shifting allegiances and oppositions of *Lamia* make it difficult to interpret any one character or position as corresponding to some stable value within the argument of the poem. Lamia is herself an illusion, and the poem's critique of rationality is balanced by a dramatization of the damagingly self-deluding power of the imagination.

It is nevertheless instructive to contrast the essentially elegiac manner of the passage from Keats with Shelley's quite different conception of scientific knowledge. Of all the Romantics, only Shelley – whose poetry constantly displays a knowledgeable interest in contemporary scientific ideas – makes the distinction between science and technology which frees scientific knowledge from its associations with the inhuman. Consider for example Shelley's obvious fascination with the properties of refracted and unrefracted light. This kind of concern is very characteristic of Shelley's poetry, and often makes his poetic writing into an extraordinary mingling of descriptive with analytic observation. In Act I of *Prometheus Unbound*, for instance, when a character speaks of a high mountain atmosphere as 'Thou serenest Air/Through which the Sun walks burning without beams' (I, ll. 64–5), the reference is that light is hardly refracted by a rarefied atmosphere. Conversely, in a passage from Act II, scene iii, the reference is to an atmosphere without light:

> Through the gray void abysm,
>   Down, down!
> Where the air is no prism,
> And the moon and stars are not,
> And the cavern-crags wear not
> The radiance of Heaven.
>
> (Act II, scene iii, ll. 72–7)

As a matter of fact Keats too can catch this manner of wonder in the physical properties of things, when for example he draws on his medical knowledge in the final stanza of the 'Ode to Psyche'. But it is important to note that in this particular case Keats does actually know something in a scientific way; he is thinking of the metaphors used by doctors in his day to describe the appearance of the human brain in dissection. Such precision of focus is relatively rare in the Romantics, apart from Shelley. Their rejection of science was largely conceptual, based in little real knowledge of contemporary ideas and practices.

It is worth pondering the possible causes of this principled rather than informed hostility. One crucial factor was undoubtedly the realization of the new and alarming human consequences of industrialism, registered early by Blake and widely deplored by cultural commentators in the first 30 years of the nineteenth century. The real object of the Romantics' hostility was very frequently not science strictly speaking, but science considered in the effects of its service to industrial technology. Science and industrial technology were indeed closely associated in their seminal periods of development, in England in the late seventeenth and early eighteenth century. The origins, personnel and general outlook of the Royal Society, for instance, are themselves primary material in the study of industrialization. Early nineteenth-century attitudes to science dwelt especially on its unwittingness so far as the effects of its applications were concerned. It seemed a devastating criticism that knowledge of such potential power should derive simply from the accurate description of phenomena, so as to predict their behaviour and thus manipulate them to specific purposes. Science in this greatly powerful descriptive and predictive function was an activity concerned solely with cause and effect, and not at all with questions of motive or purpose. It gave man power devoid of metaphysical content, of spiritual or ethical significance.

In terms of our own contemporary experience this indictment of science as an inherently undesirable because ethically void activity has hardly lost force. Technology had proved far worse in some of its effects than Keats would have dared imagine. The manipulative reification of nature by technology has recently been further associated, in feminist thinking, with an arid and domineering male rationalism which has, it is argued, corrupted development in a whole range of fields of knowledge, particularly since that separation of science from philosophy and the arts which characterizes the turn of the eighteenth and nineteenth centuries.

Amongst the Romantic poets, only Shelley sustained a positive perspective in the face of these crushing problems. The questions raised by technological applications of science are implicit, for example, in *Prometheus Unbound*, a poem that addresses the most difficult problems in human experience, concerning the origins of evil and the extent of human responsibility for it. *Prometheus Unbound* makes constant reference to properties of nature which are known by scientific theory rather than sensory experience, and it is clear that Shelley wished to make scientific understanding central to the scheme of his poetic drama. Why was this? For *Prometheus Unbound* is primarily a poem about social revolution, and it can be puzzling to consider, not just where and how the science comes into the poem, but why it is there at all.

Shelley's interest in science was concerned particularly with those areas at the theoretical frontier of research. The turn of the nineteenth century was a momentous and exciting period for science, especially in England, where the foundations of modern science were laid down during a half-century of intensive speculation and experimentation. The known elements proliferated and were itemized with rapidly increasing clarity. Gases were isolated and their startling properties investigated. Electricity (static, of course, not current) and magnetism were still quite recently recognized phenomena, and very imperfectly understood. The true nature of heat and light was also not understood, but attracted a great deal of speculative commentary. The central theoretical problem of the time was the difficulty of accounting for the *transformation of forces* in nature. How was it that physically remote bodies could act on each other? What was the physical explanation of causal relations between substances separated in space? The phenomena most involved in such questions – electricity, magnetism, gravity, heat, light – were grouped together and known as the 'imponderables'. They were accounted for by positing the existence of weightless substances which transmitted cause and effect relationships as material operations. In the case of heat, for example, this substance was known as 'caloric', and was held to leave a burning body as 'phlogiston'. Light, electricity and magnetism were all superfine fluids (as was caloric), moving through the medium of a superfine 'ether'. All these physical phenomena were considered to exist in one way or another as actual particles.

In the version elaborated by Adam Walker (a popular science writer and lecturer who taught Shelley at Eton), all the 'imponderables' were considered to be different forms of one substance; and this substance was present in the human body, too, and included amongst its effects the sensation of love (for here was simply an instance of a transformational force acting between separate bodies). This meant that for Shelley light, for instance, and love could be equivalent not just in the terms of a serviceable metaphor but in material fact. Electricity was particularly associated with the physical sensations of love (as was magnetism – 'animal magnetism'), and in Shelley's poetry this identification ubiquitously 'tingles', usually in the most dramatic form of static electricity then known – lightning. In short, Shelley's informed understanding of his world comprehended the assumption of a basic physical unity between humanity and the rest of nature, in that dynamic transformational forces were at play throughout all matter, human and other. An understanding then of the laws governing such forces was obviously indispensable to social change. More than this, dynamic change in nature – the short-term destruction and long-term fertility of volcanic activity, say – could be symbolic of change in the human order, but symbolic in Coleridge's sense; it could be understood as itself a part of the larger change for which it was a symbol.

It is not surprising that processes and routines of work made possible by scientific advance should have invited concern. The passage from Southey's *Letters from England*, already discussed above, brings home the sense of shock and moral outrage caused by the new modes of production in the early nineteenth century. It is interesting to note that Robert Southey, who had in the mid-1790s been a fiercely extremist radical (and close friend of Coleridge in his radical phase), had, by 1807, moved in a representative way towards a political outlook of marked conservative reaction. Southey represents here an early version of what is to become a consistent feature of the intellectual right in English cultural debate. The alarming social conditions created by industrialism are forcefully deplored, and are associated with progressive social elements: democracy, for example; mass civilization, with its besetting vices of manipulative mass-media and advertising; the collapse of immemorial social hierarchies, based in the land and – so the argument goes – in touch with the rhythms of nature. Many influential cultural commentators have subsequently developed a critique of English social life founded in these assumptions of an almost irresistible drive towards annihilation of a stable, land-based social order. Indeed the views on these matters of such writers and critics as Matthew Arnold, T.S. Eliot, and F.R. Leavis have become inseparable from a whole dominant reading of English literature in its social relations which has governed academic representations of Romanticism for more than a century. These anxieties, spawned by the effects of industrialism on the quality of human life, are not in the least allayed by events and developments in the troubled years after 1815.

· THREE ·
The post-war period: after 1815

The social tensions which became apparent in English society with the breakdown of the wartime consensus were so acute that they produced an atmosphere of imminent domestic crisis more serious even than anything experienced in the 1790s.

There had been sporadic outbreaks of industrial violence and other signs of discontent during the war years, amongst those workers whose way of life had been disrupted by the economic effects of the war (combined with various other effects of deeper changes in the markets and structures of British industries). Napoleon's 'Continental System', an effort to block the lines of communication of British exports, had been exacerbated in its effects by the retaliatory 'Orders in Council' restricting foreign trade. The weaving and lace industries, in Yorkshire and Nottinghamshire particularly, saw serious outbreaks of violence in 1811 and 1812 when (as so often in the period) bad harvests intensified grievances and distress. These 'Luddite' forms of industrial action – machine-breaking, intimidation of blacklegs and unpopular employers – re-emerged after 1815 as part of a larger pattern of widespread discontent and vocal anti-government feeling. The English 'working class' was not yet aware of itself as a significantly homogeneous social group, although its development as such was an integral feature of the new intensive modes of production. But its presence was first felt in the years of political and social ferment between Waterloo and the Reform of 1832.

The unpopularity of Lord Liverpool's Tory government grew towards the end of the second decade of the nineteenth century. Its power base had become uncertain in the conflict of an established landed interest with the new economic power of the mercantile and industrial capitalists. It also countered the apparent threat of revolution with a considerable extension of the domestic spy system developed during Pitt's ministry. The leading figures in the government were much criticized and abused outside their own social circles. Castlereagh, as Foreign Secretary, had been an architect of the new European balance of power agreed by the victorious powers at the Congress of Vienna in 1815. France had been neutralized by a ring of 'buffer' states designed to contain its continuing revolutionary threat. The cost of this arrangement was the stimulation of several European nationalist movements on the part of groups who felt their own country or people slighted in the disposition of boundaries or the presence of occupying forces. Byron and Shelley, in fact, became quite closely involved in the Italian version of this radical nationalism (the 'Carbonari' movement) during their years of exile. They also followed closely other liberation movements in southern Europe, in Spain, for example, and in Greece, where the struggle for freedom was to cost Byron his life. It is very noticeable as a consequence that the more directly topical poetry of Shelley and Byron displays a special hostility towards Castlereagh, the Foreign Secretary who embodied (in his way actually quite skilfully) imperialist, reactionary post-war England for the rest of Europe. The powerful personal and political attack on Castlereagh in the 'Dedication' to Byron's *Don Juan* – so powerful, indeed, that it was omitted from the poem's first edition in 1819, and not thereafter published until 1833 – gives very vividly the animated loathing which the second generation Romantics reserved for 'the intellectual eunuch':

> Cold-blooded, smooth-faced, placid miscreant!
>   Dabbling its sleek young hands in Erin's gore,
> And thus for wider carnage taught to pant,
>   Transferred to gorge upon a sister shore,
> The vulgarest tool that tyranny could want,
>   With just enough of talent and no more,
> To lengthen fetters by another fixed
> And offer poison long already mixed.
>
> An orator of such set trash of phrase,
>   Ineffably, legitimately vile,
> That even its grossest flatterers dare not praise,
>   Nor foes – all nations – condescend to smile.
> Not even a sprightly blunder's spark can blaze
>   From that Ixion grindstone's ceaseless toil,
> That turns and turns to give the world a notion
> Of endless torments and perpetual motion.
>
> A bungler even in its disgusting trade,
>   And botching, patching, leaving still behind

> Something of which its masters are afraid,
>   States to be curbed and thoughts to be confined,
> Conspiracy or congress to be made,
>   Cobbling at manacles for all mankind,
> A tinkering slave-maker, who mends old chains,
> With God and man's abhorrence for its gains.
>
> (stanzas 12–14)

Shelley too offers a very great deal of direct political comment in his poetry, although only rarely does he aim for Byron's Pope-like satirical savagery. Shelley's perspectives tend to be longer term and more idealist in spirit, though they are none the less exact, when occasion arises, in contemporary reference and straightforward engagement with the great historical issues which were played out around him in Europe in the first quarter of the century. Such poems as the 'Ode to Liberty', which was published together with *Prometheus Unbound* in 1820, are even structured around historical analysis of political change in Europe. But Shelley always understands particular events in the context of underlying principles and forces for change; as in his sonnet now known as 'To the Republic of Benevento' (originally published posthumously by Mary Shelley as 'Political Greatness'). The poem reflects upon a failed Carbonari uprising of 1820 in a small town near Naples:

> Nor happiness, nor majesty, nor fame,
> Nor peace, nor strength, nor skill in arms or arts
> Shepherd those herds whom Tyranny makes tame:
> Verse echoes not one beating of their hearts,
> History is but the shadow of their shame –
> Art veils her glass, or from its pageant starts
> As to Oblivion their blind millions fleet
> Staining that Heaven with obscene imagery
> Of their own likeness. – What are numbers knit
> By force or custom? Man who man would be,
> Must rule the empire of himself; in it
> Must be supreme, – establishing his throne
> On vanquished will, – quelling the anarchy
> Of hopes and fears, – being himself alone. –

This unflinching insistence on the real difficulty of social revolution recognizes that minds must undergo radical change before actions and institutions can embody any permanent transformation. Such intellectual honesty is central in Shelley's political poetry. It is a tempering realism, always restraining and modifying the idealizing thrust of his political vision, which was enforced for Shelley by the social–historical lessons of his own experience.

Shelley shared Byron's loathing of Castlereagh, but he had more personal reasons for despising the Lord Chancellor, Eldon. Eldon had deprived Shelley of the custody of his children after the suicide of his first wife. But Eldon was anyway unpopular in the country generally, because, like Castlereagh (somewhat unjustly) and Sidmouth, the Home Secretary, his name was associated with the Tory government's aggressively repressive policies against social unrest and public disturbances.

The troubles were brought to a focus in August 1819 by the Peterloo massacre, by far the worst of a number of incidents in which disproportionate legal and military force was used to combat radical activity that was generally peaceful. At Peterloo a nervous local magistracy called in troops to disperse a huge but peaceful meeting at St Peter's Fields in Manchester that had gathered to hear 'Orator' Henry Hunt, a popular radical lecturer. In the resulting cavalry charge and panic 11 people lost their lives and over 400 were injured (Plate 8). The news of the massacre (named 'Peterloo' on analogy with Waterloo) caused a national furore which served only to strengthen the government's resolve. It also stung Shelley, who received the news in Italy a few weeks after the event, into writing *The Mask of Anarchy*, perhaps the greatest English poem of radical political feeling. Its opening stanzas brilliantly catch the mood and manner of popular reaction by adapting the style of the political cartoonists to the ballad-like idiom of the poem:

> As I lay asleep in Italy
> There came a voice from over the Sea,
> And with great power it forth led me
> To walk in the Visions of Poesy.
>
> I met Murder on the way –
> He had a mask like Castlereagh,
> Very smooth he looked, yet grim;
> Seven bloodhounds followed him:
>
> All were fat, and well they might
> Be in admirable plight,
> For one by one and two by two
> He tossed them human hearts to chew
> Which from his wide cloak he drew.
>
> Next came Fraud, and he had on
> Like Eldon, an ermined gown;
> His big tears, for he wept well,
> Turned to millstones as he fell,
>
> And the little children who
> Round his feet played to and fro,

Plate 8 George Cruikshank, 'Massacre at St Peter's, or 'Britons Strike Home!!!', 1819

> Thinking every tear a gem,
> Had their brains knocked out by them.
>
> Clothed with the Bible, as with light,
> And the shadows of the night,
> Like Sidmouth next, Hypocrisy
> On a crocodile rode by.
>
> And many more Destructions played
> In this ghastly masquerade,
> All disguised even to the eyes
> Like Bishops, lawyers, peers and spies.
>
> (ll. 1–29)

The Gillrayesque quality here is, though, also very strikingly Shelleyan, in the telling technique of making the contemporary politicians who are named appear as the very essence and type of the evils they represent; such that, for example, the abstraction Murder is said to resemble Castlereagh, rather than the other way round, as if Murder were just an instance of the larger evil embodied in the Foreign Secretary.

The years of revolutionary threat and social disorder saw a heightened awareness of the distress that was an inevitable corollary of the changing economy. The old centres of production, with their established ways of life, were rapidly changing in character with the phenomenon of the industrial revolution. The political order also had to change, but the emergent form of English political life was difficult to predict. Shelley and Byron both considered active political involvement as an alternative to poetry, but the received political order of their class and radical creed – within the oppositional parliamentary wing of the Whig Lords – had ceased to have any effective role in the social configuration of the second decade. The period from 1815 to 1832 is marked by uncertainty, apprehension, and yet also (in spite of some lurches of the economy towards 'slump' conditions, as in the 'crash' of 1825) by an over-arching pattern of economic boom. There was a suddenly widening gap between the 'bourgeoisie', those who had successfully thrown in their lot with the values and mores of the mercantile capitalist order, and the very large productive or dispossessed class, whose interests were fundamentally at odds with those of the economically ascendant class.

All three of the major second-generation Romantic poets were alive to this vertiginous sense of change and sharp conflict in society. It is an essential feature of their importance that they address this social experience so directly, and with such profound and passionate engagement. It is no fault of theirs – it is no accident either – that their characteristic concern with society, and with history, has been much distorted and much obscured. The very word 'Romantic' has itself played an interesting part in the blurring of subsequent critical perspectives on the Romantic poets; but this point raises issues more appropriately dealt with at the end of this book.

It is now possible to place the Romantic poets more exactly in the context provided by the preceding outline of events and characteristics in each period. It will, however, be helpful first briefly to note some pertinent similarities and differences between the precise historical moments of the first- and second-generation poets.

Both generations lived, of course, in the shadow of the French Revolution. But the experience of this Revolution was very different for each generation. Blake, Wordsworth and Coleridge lived through the initial surge of excitement and optimism. They also lived through the collapse of this millenial optimism, and were then caught in the loyalist wartime backlash against English radicalism and its sympathy with French principles. Under the pressure of the war years and the development of educated English opinion towards conservative cultural insularity, the first-generation poets either drifted into relative obscurity and eccentricity, or found themselves moving with the tide towards an affirmation of political and religious orthodoxy.

By the end of the Napoleonic wars these poets, and especially Wordsworth, represented for a new generation the most craven and disreputable apostasy. Keats, Shelley and Byron could look back to the still quite recent spectacle of the Revolution, and find its principles a continuing source of political idealism and inspiration. They had not, however, experienced the vicious backlash of the 1790s and the war; their democratic values had not been called upon to survive that kind of shock. In the climate of rapid change and new initiatives, and against a background of very widespread social unrest, the younger poets could address themselves in the post-war years to the great issues of change in the state – to the struggle for 'Liberty' – in a spirit once more positive.

It is a truism that all periods of history turn out on some terms or other to be periods of great change and crisis. But there is no doubt that the period of the Romantics was considered *at the time* to be a momentous epoch. The Revolution was interpreted by its friends and its enemies as an absolute break with the past. Wordsworth's own detailed and sustained account of it in *The Prelude* makes this perfectly clear. It seems then reasonable to anticipate an unusual proportion of relatively direct social and political content in the work of the Romantics.

It is necessary, however, to enter a question about the nature and extent of such content in Romantic poetry. There is a long and powerful critical tradition which reads the Romantics as the most subjective and, so to speak, the most 'escapist' of English poets. The Romantics' pervasive concern with introspection and private consciousness, and with a nature ostensibly remote from human society, at least appears to offer strong support for such a reading. It is remarkable in one sense just how limited the impact of their contemporary world appears to have been on the Romantic poets.

But this kind of reading is partly a matter of the critical perspective that is brought to bear on their work. *The Prelude* can be read in a way which emphasizes the poet's memories of subjective experience; but it can with at least equal validity be read as an account of subjective and other kinds of experience that are all qualified by their structural relation to Wordsworth's account of the French Revolution, as a public and a personal event. For the Revolution stands in *The Prelude* between the adult Wordsworth who remembers, and the younger person whose experience of nature forms the subject of memory. The personal development is thus fused with an intervening experience of more general social crisis which dramatizes Wordsworth's varying relations with nature and with other people.

The poetry of Keats has often been interpreted as an example of a 'typically Romantic' subjective recoil from the pain, ugliness and transience of actual human experience. Keat's medievalism, his association of poetry with dreaming, with drugs or alcohol, or even with peaceful death, all seem to point towards some intense desire to shelter from reality in a visionary realm of the imagination. The historian E. P. Thompson, for example, in some cogent remarks at the beginning of his critical biography of William Morris, asserts that Keats's poetry is 'a refuge from a reality which he felt to be unbearably hostile.' In his awareness and representation of 'the acute tension between the richness of the life of the senses and imagination and the poverty of everyday experience', Thompson argues, Keats sets against the real world another 'world of art and beauty' which becomes '*more* real than life itself.'

But careful attention to the terms of the oppositions in Keats's work discovers an alertly analytical and critical representation of those orders of experience that might seem, at first, to be opposed to the everyday world and favourably contrasted with it. Is Porphyro, for example, so innocent of worldly guile, of a certain pragmatic grappling with the reality of given circumstances, in *The Eve of St Agnes*? And is Madeline, in the same poem, not represented as having a good deal to learn of the proportionate relations of imaginative idealism and physical fulfilment? Isabella and Lorenzo, the apparently over-sentimentally drawn lovers of *Isabella: or the Pot of Basil*, appear by the admittedly grotesque closing stanzas to be culpably vulnerable, heedlessly unguarded in their mutual and self-blinding absorption. And in the Odes, especially, we are returned insistently to the real world by Keats's language of sensory pleasure as the means to evoke states of intensely desirable imaginative consciousness; such states are then rooted in the direct stimuli of the material world:

> I cannot see what flowers are at my feet,
>   Nor what soft incense hangs upon the boughs,
> But, in embalmed darkness, guess each sweet
>   Wherewith the seasonable month endows
> The grass, the thicket, and the fruit-tree wild –
>   White hawthorn, and the pastoral eglantine;
>   Fast-fading violets covered up in leaves;
>   And mid-May's eldest child,
>   The coming musk-rose, full of dewy wine,
>   The murmurous haunt of flies on summer eves.
>   ('Ode to a Nightingale', ll. 41–50)

This scene, where Keats may imagine himself at one with the nightingale of his yearning, is no realm of pure imagination. It is a place of direct sensuous apprehensions, existing in space and time, and caught in an unremitting flux which always, in Keats's poetry, ironizes the moment of intense ideal experience as its artistic representation attempts to freeze it out of time.

Keats's poetry is undoubtedly 'Romantic' in a characteristic way; and what is characteristic in his work is its positive imaginative engagement with the pain of experience. In Keats's poetry (and here too he is representative) visionary experience at once returns us to the order of social reality, but in a changed attitude of mind.

PART TWO

The social relations of the Romantic poets

· FOUR ·
Blake, Wordsworth, Coleridge

Most of the articulate radical opinion in England in the 1790s centred on a small group of Dissenting and atheist intellectuals based in London. An enterprising radical publisher named Joseph Johnson provided one point of focus for this rather diffuse group. William Godwin, generally admired by English radicals after the appearance of his *Political Justice* in 1793, provided another overlapping focal point. William Blake seems to have been quite closely connected with these intellectuals, and indeed his early, very odd work 'An Island in the Moon' (1784-5) includes strange caricatures of various personalities who figured in this cultural formation. It is not suprising that Blake, a highly intelligent man whose work brought him constantly into contact with publishers and the literary scene (he of course earned his living as an engraver), and one with advanced political and religious views, should find his way to the company of such people as Godwin and Mary Wollstonecraft, Tom Paine, and radical writers and lecturers such as John Thelwall and Thomas Holcroft.

Coleridge, and to a lesser extent Wordsworth, were also at the margins of this group, and they were in contact as well with various provincial connections of the metropolitan intellectuals. Unlike Blake, whose origins were effectively in the London working class, the two poets who were to collaborate so fruitfully throughout the 1790s were both children of reasonably well-educated and comfortable middle-class families. Wordsworth's father was an attorney in Cumberland, Coleridge's a vicar in a Devonshire village; both went to Cambridge (but never met there), which was markedly more radical in outlook than conservative Oxford; both then lived in the West Country, more or less at leisure to travel (often to London) and write.

It is instructive to consider briefly the financial arrangements under which these writers actually lived in the 1790s, when their most influential and important work was produced. At this time a skilled worker such as a printer might expect to earn between £80 and £100 in a year. An artist–artisan like Blake was obliged to work extremely long hours, at the exhausting and minutely demanding task of copy–engraving, in order to earn anything remotely approaching that kind of sum. And, needless to say, Blake had no other source of income, throughout his life, apart from his own labour. Coleridge and Wordsworth, each with dependents to support, lived on scarcely more than this for most of the time, although they did not earn it all by their labour. Like other writers of the period they relied to an extent on the informal private patronage of admiring friends and acquaintances. One such patron, Raisley Calvert, left Wordsworth a legacy of £900 in 1795, enough in itself to yield £50 and more in annual interest. Coleridge got by on similar gifts and annuities, notably from his friend and neighbour in Nether Stowey, Tom Poole, and especially from the Midlands businessman Josiah Wedgwood. He would on occasion simply present Coleridge with cash sums – sometimes of as much as £100 – and in 1798 Wedgwood 'saved' Coleridge from a post as a Unitarian minister on £120 a year by offering him an annuity of £150 in order to devote himself to poetry and philosophy.

This kind of income needs of course to be understood in comparative terms. In the early years of the nineteenth century a large proportion of the nation's wealth was concentrated in very few hands. If, following historians, we distinguish three land-owning classes in the period – the aristocracy, the gentry and a land or trade-based 'lesser gentry' – then the distribution of wealth can be quickly grasped. A family in the gentry class might expect to live on between £3,000 and £4,000 per year; about the figure, for instance, the Bingley has to live on in *Pride and Prejudice*. There were perhaps 1,000 such families in Regency England, owning between them some 15 per cent of the land. The 'lesser gentry' was more numerous – possibly 2,000 or so families – and they could expect an income of around £1,000; roughly the level of families such as the Dashwoods in *Sense and Sensibility*, or the Bennetts in *Pride and Prejudice*. Wordsworth and Coleridge came from families at the lower margins of this class. Altogether this class may have owned about 12.5 per cent of the land, and as it shaded into a still vaguer, and larger social grouping of 'country gentlemen' – possibly comprising about 10,000 families – whose income ranged upwards from about £300, the total land ownership constituted about 35 per cent of the whole.

But it has to be remembered that, over and above all these land-owning and wealthy families, there was a tiny handful of landed aristocratic families which between themselves owned at least a quarter of all land, and which were accustomed to incomes of between £5,000 and £10,000 per year, and even more. Some characters in Jane Austen, Darcy in *Pride and Prejudice*, for instance, or Rushworth in *Mansfield Park*, are in this millionaire class. All of these families, however, from the country gentlemen to the richest aristocrats, represent in total no more than two or three per cent of the population of England in the period. The vast majority of the population lived on a rural or factory wage that might have ranged between one shilling and ten shillings per week. As we shall see, these social configurations make for difficulty when writers such as Coleridge and Wordsworth attempt to speak for this great mass, and against their own social peers, who were also at that time the only audience for poetry.

The deep divisions that really underlay the initial apparent unity of radical enthusiasm for the Revolution were of a sort particularly damaging to Godwin's circle of radical intellectuals. The fragmentation of this unity, under strong social pressures that were cleverly orchestrated by the Tories, seems to have involved a polarization of suddenly more self-conscious class positions. Working-class radicalism that was based on the new industries, mainly urban, found itself opposed to an increasingly repressive political status quo. But at the level of the new relations of production which had brought this conflict into being, the radical atheists and Dissenters – the majority of them from educated and industrious Dissenting and commercial backgrounds – were very awkwardly placed. Their own social milieu was just that of the vanguard of capitalist expansion and technological advance. This milieu of London and Midland discussion groups included such people as the scientist and Unitarian Joseph Priestley, and the community of scientists and engineers and business entrepreneurs like the Wedgwood brothers, James Watt, Matthew Boulton and Samuel Galton. The radicals whose social being was formed within this particular social range were thus speaking in the 1790s for an abstract conception of 'the people', with whose real interests they could not in fact identify. Their egalitarian convictions led, with bitter irony, to a distressing isolation both from the great mass of the common people, and from their own social class, now alienated by the dangerous expression of doctrines even remotely revolutionary.

Indeed, recent research has shown that the real energies and driving spirit of English working-class radicalism went deep underground in the later 1790s and thereafter, to survive and develop in a social and cultural terrain utterly strange and even totally unknown to writers of the middle class. Working men who subscribed to the opinions of such radical activists as Thomas Spence often belonged to a sub-criminal underworld where popular print-shops shaded into illicit dealings in pornography, and where a central forum for discussion and the dissemination of ideas was the rowdy London ale-house, in all its teeming connectedness with prostitution and thievery. Many of those radical leaders who later became accepted and even respected writers and businessmen, people such as Thomas Hardy and Francis Place, themselves became alienated from this unfamiliar hidden matrix of the working-class radical culture. Certainly, Wordsworth and Coleridge and their circle were extremely unlikely to remain in touch with such a culture.

Blake, Wordsworth and Coleridge were different in their origins, but united in their shared relation to the radical–intellectual culture which was first enlivened, and then depressed and broken up, by the course of events and by the logic of its economic situation. Only Blake was old enough in 1789 to produce work of a full creative maturity in the years of revolutionary optimism. Born in 1757, he had followed the course of the American War of Independence and could respond at once to the French Revolution in terms provided by those traditions of parliamentary and religious reformism that have already been discussed. The work of Blake's early period – the *Songs of Innocence and of Experience*, the *Marriage of Heaven and Hell*, and the earlier illuminated 'prophecies' – displays an exuberance and energetic originality which is not fully sustained beyond the years of political reaction. After the mid-1790s Blake's work becomes more inaccessibly complex and private in its sources and symbolism. The sense of a possible audience appears lost, and in this respect Blake's career is consonant with those of many London radicals.

Wordsworth and Coleridge were in touch with the London radical intellectuals, but their precise social experience was differently inflected; it was rural (a setting obviously in sharp contrast to the more obviously urban basis of radical ideas), and the emergence of their creative gifts came later, in the much bleaker climate of the late 1790s. Their work, almost from its origins, is turned more to the inner resources of imagination and subjective experience than to the community at large. Indeed, as has already been suggested, this disjunction of public and private experience is a major theme in Wordsworth, and in Coleridge too. Coleridge's desire to constitute a surrogate community of friends and family, in a nature unspoilt by society, took early theoretical form in his plan for a 'Pantisocracy' on the banks of the Susquehanna river in Pennsylvania. The same desire underlies the art of the 'conversation poems' such as 'This Lime-Tree Bower my Prison' and 'Frost at Midnight'. And in his much underrated poem 'Fears in Solitude', another work in the conversational idiom, Coleridge achieves complex effects of tone in a particularly interesting combination of directly political reflection with the characteristically 'private' meditative manner of the best conversation poems.

The negative side of Coleridge's social experience can be discerned in that range of feelings – isolation, the consequences of unwitting

Plate 9 James Gillray, 'The New Morality', 1798

transgression, the desperate need for an audience and a meaningful relation to the community – which contribute to the uncanny power of *The Ancient Mariner*.

Wordsworth's and Coleridge's specific experience of social hostility, during the years in which the first *Prelude*, the *Lyrical Ballads*, and the 'conversation poems' were written, was at times unnervingly direct. The two poets were actually spied on by Home Office agents on the Quantocks in 1798, and local hostility towards the 'damned Jacobins' eventually drove Wordsworth and his sister Dorothy out of their home, 'Alfoxden', near Coleridge's cottage in Nether Stowey. Coleridge, Southey, Charles Lamb and other liberal writers were also attacked in print in the late 1790s, most damagingly in a satirical print by Gillray entitled 'The New Morality' (Plate 9) which appeared in the pro-government magazine, the *Anti-Jacobin* (1798).

· FIVE ·
Keats, Shelley, Byron

The three major second-generation Romantic poets all died young, and in dramatic circumstances. Keats died of 'consumption' in February 1821, soon after leaving England for Italy in a forlorn effort to retrieve his health. He was just 25. Shelley drowned in a storm off the Italian coast in 1822, aged 29. Byron died of a fever in 1824 at the age of 36 while campaigning against the Turks in the cause of Greek independence. Byron had by that time already become a legendary figure throughout Europe, but Shelley and Keats died in relative obscurity. None of these poets lived long enough to age into compromise with English society (which is not to suggest that this is what would necessarily have happened). They all died in embittered estrangement from their native country, and in each case the estrangement was a result of the political conflicts which pervaded every sphere of English life, including, perhaps most of all, the sphere of literary culture.

The case of Keats will be considered in some detail later. It will be sufficient at this point to say that his supposed lowly origins, and his association with the so-called 'Cockney School' of poetry led by the radical poet and journalist Leigh Hunt, made Keats a target for right-wing reviewers whose treatment of the poet was widely believed at the time to have resulted in his death. The generosity and kindliness which pervade Keats's marvellous letters are qualities all the more admirable for their context in Keats's brief and increasingly difficult and disheartening life. He came in fact from what might now be called a lower-middle-class background – his family had some money, but remained quite close to their origins in the service trades – and he had to struggle hard to make his way as an apprentice in the medical profession. This used up what money he had, although there was a tragic misunderstanding in Keats's financial affairs which prevented him from realizing a significant part of the income rightfully his (the problem derived ultimately from the early loss of both parents, and the appointment of imperfectly efficient and solicitous guardians). When he finally turned away from the medical training to which he had effectively committed his fortunes, in favour of a poet's calling about which he always felt some uncertainty and self-doubt, Keats's literary vocation was exceptionally difficult to sustain in the simple material sense, let alone in the circumstances of family misfortune, ill-health and vicious critical vilification which surrounded him in the three years or so of his active poetic career. When in the Nightingale Ode we read of 'The weariness, the fever, and the fret,/Here, where men sit and hear each other groan' (ll. 23–4), Keats is invoking no easy idle dreamer's conception of ordinary life, but a real and inescapable context of the poet's work.

Neither Shelley nor Byron could have been accused of having lowly origins. Byron inherited a title and the estate of Newstead Abbey (with other valuable properties) at the age of ten. Shelley was heir to a baronetcy in the Whig interest of the Duke of Norfolk. Both poets frequently displayed an almost haughty indifference to the English bourgeois values and conventions which they so readily flouted. Wordsworth, Coleridge and Keats all struggled to maintain a reasonable standard of living while devoting most of their time to writing that was not financially rewarding. Coleridge in particular was driven to desperate habits by the incessant requirements of deadline-dominated journalism and commissioned writing. Shelley and Byron, in strong contrast, lived with the freedom and mobility to which the aristocracy were well accustomed, though they did it by borrowing massively against the security of future income, at terrifying rates of interest. Shelley especially was generous to a fault with money, lending freely to those who needed or, as for example in the case of his father-in-law Godwin, to those who asked; but Shelley unluckily often gave more than he could afford, and indeed more than he had, and he also displayed a nobleman's indifference to tradesmen's bills, and to debt in general. But the tone and thematic development of Shelley's poetry, and of Byron's, was none the less determined by the social relations which characterized their position in English society.

Byron was seriously contemplating a career in politics just at the time of the phenomenal success of the first two Cantos of *Childe Harold's Pilgrimage* in March 1812. He gave two speeches in the House of Lords, one of them on the controversial topic of Catholic emancipation. The other speech was on the Luddite disturbances; Byron's Nottinghamshire estate was in the very centre of the most troubled area, surrounded by the villages of Kirkby-in-Ashfield, Blidworth and Redhill. His speech in defence of the Luddites is justly celebrated, although it is possible to overstress its originality and boldness, and it is interesting to examine the circumstances of Byron's famous speech more closely than is usual. These circumstances illuminate the real difficulty of the aristocratic writer's social and political orientation in Regency England.

The received view of Byron's speech on the Luddite frame-breakers has been that in it he enunciated a strong humanitarian commitment which took him at once well to the left of the moderate parliamentary Whigs led by Lord Holland. Byron's politics, it has been argued, were from the start too boldly out of any party line, and too close in sympathy to the sufferings of the people at large, to meet with any sustained conventional political success. But it is possible to suggest a somewhat different interpretation.

There is a crucial sense in which Byron was driven by the available idioms of political commitment and expression to a position in which any effective relationship with 'the people' was impossible. Byron's personal potentialities were constrained at the deepest level by the larger, impersonal forces of society which bore upon him as their agent. Newstead Abbey was at the very centre of Luddite activity in Nottinghamshire in November and December of 1811. The towns and villages involved – Sutton-in-Ashfield, Kirby, Bulwell, Arnold, Basford, Eastwood, Heanor – literally encircled the abbey, and some were no more than five miles away. Byron was actually at Newstead from early August to mid-October (he had just returned from his first tour of the eastern Mediterranean), and he was there again from late December into January. These periods exactly coincide with Luddite activity very close to Newstead (for example at Basford and Bulwell on 3 January). The Nottinghamshire newspapers were full of it, although significantly it appears that Byron was not following their stories carefully; his Lords speech remarks on new machinery as the cause of local unemployment, but this was flatly contradicted by the *Nottingham Review* for 6 December.

Byron's speech to the Lords on Thursday 27 February assumes as a matter of course that unemployment had been caused by the introduction of new technology. This suggests that Byron's views owed more to official Whig policy than to personal knowledge and involvement, even though Byron stresses, in his speech and in private correspondence with Lord Holland, that the personal dimension was important. In fact the whole of Byron's speech reiterates points already made in the course of Whig opposition to the Bill in the Commons and the Lords (compare for instance Hutchinson's speech in the Commons against the third reading on Thursday 20 February; a performance in many ways more politically astute than Byron's a week later).

We must briefly identify here some general characteristics of the moderate Foxite Whigs, and their position in 1812. They were, as we have already noted, Constitutionalists, with a fundamental commitment to the essential value of the freedom of the individual as the goal of political action. Since the French Revolution, they had stood for parliamentary reform, and for the defence of civil and religious liberties (and hence for Catholic emancipation; Byron's other theme in his Lords speeches). They also stood for the freedom of the press; for peace and understanding with Bonaparte; for a reduction in the political interest of the Crown. But the Whigs were, above all, an aristocratic party, in the tradition of Constitutionalism rather than democratic innovation, and in the many independent fortunes amongst its membership and leadership, historically essential in resisting 'the blandishments of the Crown'. Byron, in the whole range of his social attitudes and manners, and in his political views at this time, was very close indeed to the aristocratic moderate Foxite Whigs of the Upper House, led by Lord Holland. In spite of his own earlier attack on Lord Holland in *English Bards and Scotch Reviewers* (1809), and in spite also of the broadly Tory associations of Byron's early literary career (he sides with Pope, and with Gifford of the Tory *Quarterly Review* against the Whiggish *Edinburgh Review*), it was still to Lord Holland that Byron turned for advice about his speech against the death penalty for convicted Luddite activists.

In the speech itself Byron assumes throughout that the state legislature is the only effective and the only possible source of action; there is nothing revolutionary in its rhetoric. Economic distress is emphasized as the understandable cause of social discontent, and this economic distress is repeatedly blamed on 'the times' (i.e. the effects on trade of bad harvests, and of the Orders in Council, war with the USA, and Napoleon's continental blockade, compounded by the collapse of the false market in hosiery created by military investment). Byron insists that unemployment has been created by new machines, and he rather sentimentally castigates the poor quality of wide framework of the sort which has thrown excess output into the industries in question. The underlying cause of all these problems is identified as war. The speech also tries hard to make the military and police appear ridiculous; it laments the failure to hold a proper government enquiry into the hosiery and lace trades and their distress; it plays on the dangers of provoking a revolution; it is anti-war again on the situation in Portugal; it comes down against the death penalty itself as inefficacious as a deterrent, and as counter-productive in discouraging voluntary witnesses. Each and every one of these arguments had been used already by the Whigs in the series of debates that had already taken place on the question of the Luddites. It is only Byron's elaborate ironies, and his rather theatrical displays of sympathy for the discontented workers, which distinguish his contribution, and lead it towards the manner of a more decidedly radical position such as that of Sir Francis Burdett.

Byron soon relinquished the effort to get his political career moving, partly no doubt because he was caught up in the social round of his lionization in London after the success of *Childe Harold* and of his 'Turkish Tales' which rapidly followed. But there may in fact have been a more astute reading of the political scene behind Byron's withdrawal. The aristocratic Whigs had by the end of the war all but lost any substantial base of interest in the country at large. They could not, for example, sensibly give wholehearted and active support to a movement such as the Luddites: their own true interests, as landowners and entrepreneurs, would have been too plainly at odds with the political sentiment. In this respect the Holland House Whigs with whom Byron associated in his London years were similar to the radical intellectuals of the 1790s; they had no future in the unfolding political and economic logic of their situation. We have remarked that Wordsworth's developing self-absorption and lonely imaginative independence can be understood as a history with a larger context in his life in English society. It is equally possible to see the evolution of the Byronic hero — a personality beyond social claim and obligation, proudly lonely and aloof, brooding on some irremediable wrong or guilt – as a creation with its appropriate bearings in the precise inflection of Byron's actual social experience.

Byron's estrangement from society was exacerbated by scandal in his private life, involving several kinds of sexual delinquency and the ill-favour produced by his impatience with norms of polite behaviour. The brilliant satirical manner of *Don Juan* represents the culmination of Byron's disaffection with English society; it is a manner exactly calculated to aggrieve and offend those very bourgeois values that had driven him into exile.

Shelley too was driven into exile, though not in circumstances of celebrity and public scandal. He made himself notorious by the simple and direct persistence of his political and personal conduct, both of them radical in what was then an extreme degree. Like Wordsworth and Coleridge he suffered the attentions of government undercover agents; one of his servants was imprisoned for distributing subversive material. Like Byron he ignored or defied conventions of sex and marriage; unlike Byron, he never seriously considered a career in conventional parliamentary politics, though he could, had he wished, have taken up a seat in parliament. Byron's more extravagant expressions of radical commitment tend to come in the years of exile, in cavalier letters to his friends back at home. Shelley was a fiery rebel from his schooldays (he memorably and courageously refused to accept the institutionalized bullying at Eton College), and he was expelled from University College, Oxford, after only one term, for writing and circulating a sceptical pamphlet on the evidences of Christianity. He worked enthusiastically in the cause of democracy and the common people, in Wales and in Ireland, before leaving to escape the threat of persecution for his activities and writings. His poetry, like Byron's, but in a more thorough-going and intellectually sophisticated way, was always written in a spirit of defiant opposition to the established order in England.

· PART THREE ·

· SIX ·

The literary scene

The literary scene in England at the beginning of the nineteenth century, in which the Romantic poets worked and published, had numerous effects not only on the poets' sense of their audience and their social role and identity, but even in some ways on the actual forms and substance of their poetry.

Blake's enterprise of 'illuminated printing', which he began in the later 1780s, is particularly interesting in its relation to wider changes in the publishing and bookselling trades which were taking place in the late eighteenth and early nineteenth centuries. Blake combined an extraordinary range of creative abilities in his virtually single-handed productions of illustrated poetry, such as *Songs of Innocence and of Experience*. For this work he was author, printer, illustrator, engraver, publisher and bookseller; and in this venture he exemplifies two contrary lines of development on the entrepreneurial side of his literary milieu.

In the book trade (as in so many others) methods of production were becoming increasingly specialized in the later eighteenth century, and involved a correspondingly greater division of labour. England had become a serious force in the European book trade for the first time in the eighteenth century, and this development had included the growth of securely established native type-founding and paper-making businesses on a large scale. The book trade at the end of the eighteenth century was still largely confined to London, although there were provincial operations of note, including for example Joseph Cottle in Bristol, who launched Wordsworth and Coleridge in their public careers, and who published the first edition of *Lyrical Ballads* in 1798. Scotland, where Edinburgh had long established itself as one of the great European cities, had a quite separately thriving and complex publishing trade and associated activities.

At around the turn of the century the engineer William Nicholson took out a patent for a printing machine. From this moment the age of the hand printing press was doomed. Since the origins of European printing, books had been made from hand-set type, and hand-printed sheets of paper (made from a variety of waste materials including large amounts of rags and rope). The method could produce printed books of great beauty and extraordinary durability, but it was slow, arduous and expensive. The onset of mechanization was an essential feature in other social developments of an ostensibly different kind; the great increase in a literate population generated a demand for books totally beyond the productive capacity which had served for centuries. As it turned out, the new machinery proved useless without the rapid evolution of new techniques across the range of related industries. New ways of making paper were quickly developed. Mechanization in this area too was inevitable (the first machine was introduced in 1799). The new technology drew also on new materials, notably wood pulp. This, together with the demand for ship-timber in the Napoleonic period, was to have momentous results for the remaining wild woodland of England. But there was no alternative, if new production methods were to be realized. The first practical paper-making machines were in operation by 1803, and as output rose at bewildering speed – it increased tenfold in just two or three years – so prices fell and the market was transformed. One important motivating force behind the pressure for change was the steeply rising demand for newspapers, and in particular for the increasingly influential and widely read London *Times*.

Blake, in his work as a professional engraver, would have experienced directly the growing power of the publisher. There had been a decisive change, by the early years of the nineteenth century, from the eighteenth-century pattern of major literary figures surrounded by an admiring and commercially eager throng of publisher–booksellers. The situation was now almost reversed, in fact. Artists, like writers, could no longer depend for commissions on aristocratic patronage, as they had done in former times. We have already seen how writers such as Wordsworth and Coleridge were caught awkwardly, in this respect, in the transition from one set of structures and practices to another. Authors were now coming to depend, in the words of an historian, on 'the anonymous patronage of the public who purchased on a large scale.' The painter and the engraver were becoming 'producers whose productions were retailed by the publisher.' The engraver in particular found his artistic independence threatened in his role as the publisher's commissioned intermediary between the painter and the public. One central purpose behind Blake's project of illustrated poems was to achieve an immediacy of relationship with his audience, in which absolute control over the nature of the finished product was essential. The result was a series of books of astonishing beauty and originality. But as a publishing venture they could not succeed. New market conditions and new facts of literary life ensured that Blake's magnificent attempt to reach his audience without the publisher's mediation was too much against the current of the times.

In a different sense, however, Blake's career runs quite plainly with that current. His bold and imaginative individual initiative was exactly in the spirit of a new generation of publishers whose methods introduced new factors into the career of writing. Amongst the 'revolutionary' practices introduced by publishers at this time were no-credit, cash-only sales, and also the practice of 'remaindering' unsold copies of a book which had been over-printed, at greatly reduced price (James Lackington first introduced this practice in the early years of the century; it has of course since become universal).

Blake was many decades ahead of his time in thinking of the author as the most important person in the production and distribution of literature. Copyright itself had not existed in practice before 1710, and many publishers retained *de facto* copyright until the 1760s. Throughout the eighteenth century the bookseller had remained the key figure in the literary culture. His shop, often combined with a coffee-house, had provided the typical focus for literary coteries and the meeting of minds. Different booksellers usually combined to meet the cost of substantial new publications, and shared in the profits of their common ventures. Much serious writing was thus financed by the undertaking of a communal risk. Together with the subscription list – a way of financing a book by guaranteed advance sales at a good price – literature was produced and distributed in a context where the value of the writing was assumed in advance and secured in financial terms by the co-operation of the whole literary culture.

By the beginning of the nineteenth century the situation had changed. Growing competition for a quickly expanding readership drove the most flourishing booksellers towards a transformation into the form of the characteristic nineteenth- and twentieth-century publishing houses. It was at this time that the whole book trade assumed the three-part structure – publishers-wholesaler, printer, retail bookseller – which has subsequently remained basically in place. With the emergence of the first great publishers came the criterion of large sales as an index of literary success. And with the development of this criterion the Romantic poets were provided with an unhappy register of their public standing and influence.

Mention has already been made of William Hazlitt's *Spirit of the Age*, which so brilliantly characterizes English society of the period as a complex amalgam of oppositions whose terms constantly overlap to create perplexing cultural contradictions and paradoxes. The new publishing world of the early nineteenth century was an integral part of that culture, and its structure also has such oppositional and contradictory characteristics. Four great publishers had emerged by the beginning of the nineteenth century. Two of them, Thomas Longman and John Murray, were based in London; the other two, Archibald Constable and William Blackwood, were based in Edinburgh. Friendships and the natural community of interests amongst these firms were qualified by commercial rivalry, political oppositions and a set of broader polarities (North against South, Scottish against English, provincial against metropolitan), which all worked to create the special atmosphere of conflict and opposition in which the world of publishing is enveloped throughout the period. Cool and dispassionate judgements of literary merit, on the first appearance of any work, were simply out of the question. Far too much was always at stake to allow credit to the other side, and no kind of publication had any real choice other than to take sides. In short, publishing conditions were not exempt from the general cultural consequences of the French Revolution and its aftermath – heightened conflicts of principle, the inescapably political implications of word and action – just as the driving individualistic endeavour behind the expansion of the trade was part of a larger movement of economic growth and success.

The implications of this state of affairs for reviewing practices and the determination of literary reputations is a matter which requires separate consideration. It is, however, illuminating to note as a preliminary some features of the Romantics' publishing histories. In particular, the relatively recent criterion of high sales as a mark of success allows us to infer something of the mood and confidence of the poets, of their changing sense of an audience, and of their own purpose and calling as artists.

The contrast between Shelley and Byron is very striking in this respect. In the period just before Byron's prodigious success with the first two Cantos of *Childe Harold* early in 1812, the most successful poet of the day was Sir Walter Scott. His *Marmion* had sold 2,000 copies in the first month after its publication in 1808; in 1810 *The Lady of the Lake* sold well over 20,000 within a year. There were other instances of great commercial success by poets. Byron's close friend Thomas Moore (whose sweetly musical verses made him, with Scott and Byron, Thomas Campbell and Samuel Rogers, one of the most fashionable poets of the day) received from Longman in December 1814 an advance of £3,000 for *Lalla Rookh*, before a single word of it had been written.

Byron's success, though, was for a few years unrivalled. The reasons for the success of *Childe Harold* are in themselves very revealing of public taste in the Regency period. Discussion of the poem itself is not appropriate here, but the extent of the poem's success is clearly of great interest. *Childe Harold* was issued in March 1812 in a quarto edition of 500 copies. This edition rapidly sold out and was followed by a second edition in octavo of 3,000. Three more editions were issued before the end of the year, and more than 5,000 copies were sold in the first six months. The subsequent third and fourth Cantos of *Childe Harold* (published in 1816 and 1818 respectively) also sold very well, but the most sensational sales were those of the 'Turkish Tales', published when Byron was living in London and at the height of his fame. *The Bride of Abydos* (1813) sold 6,000 in the first month, *The Corsair* (1814), incredibly, 10,000 on the first day of publication. *Lara* (1814) and *The Siege of Corinth* (1816) each sold out first editions of 6,000 within a few weeks. This degree of popularity enters significantly into the formation of the 'Byronic' hero and personality as that of a man consciously in the glare of public gaze, and yet alienated, increasingly, from the values and the moral approval of that public. Only in *Don Juan* does the Byronic personality take up positively aggressive attitudes towards this audience, and once this happens the poetry is received as more genuinely offensive than merely fascinating.

Shelley has no consistent poetic persona of the Byronic sort, and, ironically, his whole political outlook was grounded in an at least theoretical confidence in the ability of people to change for the better. He has none of Byron's self-brooding pessimism and scorn of human society. But Shelley had no audience at all as a poet, let alone the public success of his friend Byron. Predictably, Shelley was vilified by reviewers of opposed political interest (though his publisher Charles Ollier appears to have exerted 'inside' influence on the periodical which one would have expected to attack him most, *Blackwood's Edinburgh Magazine*), but the main impression Shelley had of his own publishing career was of simple failure. This dramatized the difficulty of effecting social change by means of a mental revolution in which poetry had, in Shelley's view, a central role to play. Shelley's *Alastor*, for example, published in March 1816, is concerned to represent the dangers attendant upon poets who fail in their social responsibilities. And yet by August 1817 the publisher Ollier was writing of the book's sales as 'scarcely anything'. Shelley suffered too from censorship, as did Byron and many other radicals of the period. His epic of political revolution, *Laon and Cythna*, finally published in 1818 as *The Revolt of Islam* (this title made the political issues appear further from home), encountered considerable difficulties of this kind, and *The Mask of Anarchy* – carefully designed as it was for a popular audience – was not published in his lifetime for fear of prosecution.

Even those major works of Shelley that were intended for a small intellectual vanguard of revolution, such as *Prometheus Unbound*, encountered depressing indifference from the public at large. The *Prometheus* volume, which first appeared in 1820 and which included, in addition to the title poem, the 'Ode to Heaven', the 'Ode to the West Wind' and 'To a Sky-Lark', could be purchased in London a few years after Shelley's death, in the original edition, at a reduction of 70 per cent.

The rapid expansion in publishing was a development which implied an audience for literature that was growing with equal rapidity. How then was this new audience constituted? It is clear that the enormous growth of the population, coupled especially in the last decades of the eighteenth century with an Evangelical zeal in teaching people to read (to foster independent study of the Bible), helped to produce a huge increase in literacy. The circulation of Paine's *Rights of Man* in the 1790s, which it will be recalled may have run into millions, itself points to some such extraordinary change in the potential audience for the printed word. But this vast new audience was not the audience for poetry; the potential readership of the Romantics is a matter which calls for more careful attention.

An expanding middle class was one distinctive feature of English society. This relatively cultured and leisured social group was a product of the capitalist revolution in production. Its ascendancy opened up the market for leisure reading, particularly amongst middle-class women, and more especially in the form of novels or narrative poems that were specifically directed towards what was coming to be known (in a phrase of Coleridge's) as the 'reading public'. The phrase described an audience for literature relatively much larger than any that had existed before. It was also an extraordinarily homogeneous audience in its values and tastes. For the literary culture of early nineteenth-century England was much more generally available than it had been in earlier periods. National newspapers, magazines, reviews and other periodical publications multiplied between the 1780s and the 1830s. Standards of taste, amongst the cultivated middle class rather than the massive popular audience, were formed in these periodicals and sustained right across the whole scattered distribution of the 'reading public' by their comprehensive publication.

An important duality could then emerge within the range of English readers. There was on the one hand that incalculably vast number of common working people who could and did read, mostly political or religious works circulated in cheap forms. There was on the other hand a much more limited but still growing and remarkably unified polite reading public, whose political interests – particularly during the reactionary years of the war and its aftermath – were markedly at odds with the larger literate population. This duality gave the basic democratic impulse in, for example, *Lyrical Ballads* or Blake's *Songs*, or more obviously *The Mask of Anarchy* or Byron's *Vision of Judgment*, a paradoxical effect. Romantic poetry in its radical dimension (a dimension better understood by its contemporary readers than it has ever been since) could not reach the mass of the people, whose exclusion from adequate means to education severely limited their access to the English literary tradition. But that poetry nevertheless alienated its actual readership in a way that produced antipathetic critical responses of sometimes astonishing violence.

The range of magazines and reviews that came into being in the period once again registers the profoundly oppositional spirit and political resonance with which literary controversy and discussion was conducted. Reviews proliferated in the heated intellectual climate of the 1790s, but the most important moment in the history of periodical literature came in 1802 with the founding of the *Edinburgh Review* by a small group of young Whig intellectuals. The *Edinburgh* was published by Constable and edited by the brilliant young lawyer Francis Jeffrey as a project to revive the spirit of Whig principles in the period of their lowest fortunes and enthusiasm. Its great success led to the creation of a rival Tory review, the *Quarterly*, published from 1809 by Murray in London with close government involvement and co-operation. It was edited by William Gifford, and opposed the *Edinburgh*'s Whig bias with a deeply conservative and orthodox Anglican establishment outlook.

Reviews strictly carried only reviews of new books, though often in the form of very long and expert essays on a broad range of subjects. Magazines, however, carried miscellaneous contents including reviews but also poetry and discursive essays, correspondence, legal and political reports, and other items of interest. Their appeal was intellectually somewhat less demanding than that of the reviews, though both kinds of publication contributed to the richness and breadth of intellectual energy in the period. In 1817 the other leading Edinburgh publisher, William Blackwood, founded *Blackwood's Edinburgh Magazine*. 'Maga', as it was generally called, was a racier and more unscrupulously reactionary periodical than the *Quarterly Review*; its attacks on John Keats in the series of articles on the 'Cockney School' were only the most notorious examples of its style and prejudices, but it was none the less an extremely influential voice in the climate of opinion.

It produced in its turn – and again it is possible to discern the contours of unfolding political conflict beneath particular cultural events – a rival publication based in London that was more radical and adventurous than the *Edinburgh Review*. This was the *London Magazine*, which, first under the editorship of John Scott and on into the early 1820s, was one of the most brilliant journals of English literary history. The *London*'s contributors included William Hazlitt, Charles Lamb and Thomas De Quincey, and its editorial policy conspicuously championed the achievements of the major Romantic poets.

The various leading periodicals carried forward every kind of intellectual debate according to the dictates of their declared political interests. Such debate was now conducted for the first time on a national scale. Readers of the *Edinburgh* and the *Quarterly* participated in the great arguments of the day with a novel immediacy; in 1818 the combined circulation of the two leading reviews approached 30,000, with an actual readership which was far greater. The influence of the great reviews was extremely powerful. Success or failure in literary ventures seemed for most educated people to go virtually on the nod of the two editors, Jeffrey and Gifford.

The effects of this intensely partisan and proliferating journalism were by no means all bad. The short discursive essay, as a critical, or speculative, or above all a polemical mode, naturally flourished in these conditions and found its finest English exponents. William Hazlitt was fiercely engaged in the political argument, in the radical cause, as was his fellow radical Leigh Hunt. On the Tory side Robert Southey – much disliked for his move from a radical to a reactionary position, and rather underrated ever since – produced a staggering amount of topical and polemical prose, some of it (the observation of English social life in particular) still of great interest.

The combative or polemical idiom in English essay-writing was balanced by the development of the essay as an expression of withdrawal from conflict. This withdrawal was into an ambience of bookish, leisured self-cultivation, and an engaging blend of evocative nostalgia with reserved drollery. Charles Lamb was the greatest writer in this manner. The distinctive qualities in the English essay which he helped to form were to be as influential on subsequent generations as the polemical mode. They are also helpful in characterizing the period as one of mentally exhausting cut-and-thrust. There was a general yearning to shelter from this world, in the personal or literary past, or in the more antiquarian side of books, a comfortable connoisseurship.

The political cut-and-thrust in literary life was in fact not quite all it seemed. The champions of Whig ideals, the defenders of individual liberty and enemies of royal patronage in the columns of the *Edinburgh*, were not in reality on the side of the democratic values which had been brought into focus in the French Revolution. Bitterly opposed as the *Edinburgh* and the *Quarterly* were, there is a sense in which they speak with one voice. Genuinely disruptive interference with the social hierarchy of the nation was after all an equal threat to both parties. It is impossible indeed to miss the plainly political motives of the *Edinburgh*'s early attacks on *Lyrical Ballads*. To his educated contemporaries and social peers, the implications of Wordsworth's critical tenets and poetic practice were dangerously radical.

Francis Jeffrey's *Edinburgh* review of Southey's epic poem *Thalaba* was published in 1801, when Southey was still closely associated with the 'Lake School' of Wordsworth and Coleridge. This review was published in the very first number of the *Edinburgh*, and it begins with a general assault on the principles of the 'Lake School' manifesto, the *Lyrical Ballads*. Here a criticism which is ostensibly literary employs terms of reference which confer upon it a very obvious political force:

> Poetry has this much, at least, in common with religion, that its standards were fixed long ago, by certain inspired writers, whose authority it is no longer lawful to question . . . the author who is now before us [i.e. Southey] belongs to a *sect* of poets, that has established itself in this country within these ten or twelve years, and is looked upon, we believe, as one of its chief champions and apostles. The peculiar doctrines of this sect, it would not, perhaps, be very easy to explain; but, that they are *dissenters* from the established systems in poetry and criticism is admitted, and proved, indeed, by the whole tenor of their compositions . . . . The disciples of this school boast much of its originality, and seem to value themselves very highly, for having broken loose from the bondage of ancient authority, and re-asserted the independence of genius. Originality, however, we are persuaded, is rarer than mere alteration; and a man may change a good master for a bad one, without finding himself at all nearer to independence. That our new poets have abandoned the old models, may certainly be admitted; but we have not been able to discover that they have yet created any models of their own; and are very much inclined to call in question the worthiness of those to which they have transferred their admiration . . . . The authors of whom we are now speaking have, among them, unquestionably, a very considerable portion of poetical talent, and have, consequently, been enabled to seduce many into an admiration of the false taste (as it appears to us) in which most of these productions are composed. They constitute, at present, the most formidable conspiracy that has lately been formed against sound judgement in matters poetical . . . . Their most distinguishing symbol is undoubtedly an affectation of great simplicity and familiarity of language. They disdain to make use of the common poetical phraseology, or to ennoble their diction by a selection of fine or dignified expressions. There would be too much of *art* in this, for that great love of nature with which they are all of

them inspired; and their sentiments, they are determined, shall be indebted, for their effect, to nothing but their intrinsic tenderness or elevation. There is something very noble and conscientious, we will confess, in this plan of composition; but the misfortune is, that there are passages in all the poems that can neither be pathetic nor sublime; and that, on these occasions, a neglect of the establishments of language is very apt to produce absolute meanness and insipidity . . . . It is in [passages of narrative and description] that we are most frequently offended with low and inelegant expressions; and that the language, which was intended to be simple and natural, is found oftenest to degenerate into mere slovenliness and vulgarity.

The vocabulary Jeffrey employs to formulate his standards of good poetry has a reference as much social as aesthetic. Wordsworth and the other members of the 'Lake School' are *'dissenters* from the established systems in poetry and criticism'. Their doctrines assert 'independence', and have abandoned the 'old models' without providing coherent new ones (the echoes of Burke's account of the French revolutionaries are striking). Their 'false taste' involves a refusal to 'ennoble their diction by a selection of fine or dignified expressions.' This 'neglect of embellishment' causes the attempt to affect 'simplicity and familiarity' to founder in 'meanness and insipidity', 'low and inelegant expressions', 'mere slovenliness and vulgarity'. Jeffrey's argument in its essentials is that poetry is a form of expression only appropriate, only *possible*, to the educated and (what is the same thing) socially superior classes. He thus refuses the basic premisses of Wordsworth's Preface to *Lyrical Ballads*: that in 'low and rustic life . . . the essential passions of the heart find a better soil in which they can attain their maturity, are less under restraint, and speak a plainer and more emphatic language'; and that the language used in 'low and rustic life' is 'more permanent and . . . far more philosophical' than that produced 'under the action of social vanity'. Jeffrey rightly discerns, in this programme for a style and a subject-matter, a claim to the rights and privileges of a social elite for whom poetry had long been an exclusive possession.

The argument of the Preface to *Lyrical Ballads* is complex and demands careful study. It is nevertheless possible to propose two very broad areas of its concern which were interpreted by contemporary readers as clear extensions of the radical argument in politics. In the Preface, and in many of the poems, Wordsworth emphasizes that the expression of significant experience – like the experience itself – has subjective origins. He thus questions the existence of external, objective criteria for value and meaning. Such a shifting of the sources of authority, from the externally imposed to the humanly determined, was a highly charged proposition in the political context of 1800. Secondly, Wordsworth's democratic prescriptions for the style and subject of poetry urged the priority of common qualities and a common language. The conventional social range of poetry was not simply in need of a change; Wordsworth proposed to sweep it away.

It is not surprising, then, that when Jeffrey reviewed Wordsworth's *Poems in Two Volumes* five years later, in 1807, he saw no reason to change his earlier views. He did, however, concentrate more on what he regarded as Wordsworth's failure to write good poetry of rustic life because he confused simplicity and the natural with a merely odd or grotesque singularity. Readers will of course wish to make up their own minds about the final degree of Wordsworth's success as a poet. The point to stress here is that for influential contemporary commentators the issue was decided on the strength of fundamentally political prejudices.

Wordsworth in fact suffered the ironic fate of scorn and critical abuse of his early work for its radicalism, and then further scorn and critical abuse later, from the second-generation Romantics, for his reactionary and apostate regression.

William Hazlitt was a profound influence on the second-generation Romantics and their contemporaries, and his developing view of Wordsworth provides a most valuable insight into what were considered the poet's strengths and limitations. It is possible here only to survey briefly three assessments of Wordsworth by Hazlitt: a review of *The Excursion* which appeared in Leigh Hunt's radical weekly paper *The Examiner*; the comments on Wordsworth in the last of Hazlitt's *Lectures on the English Poets* (1818), 'On the Living Poets'; and Hazlitt's essay on Wordsworth of 1825 in *The Spirit of the Age*.

Hazlitt's review (1814) of *The Excursion* distinguishes three aspects of Wordsworth's work which are at once distinctive and limiting of his greatness. The first of these is what Hazlitt terms (in a phrase that made a particularly strong impression on the young Keats) Wordsworth's 'intense intellectual egotism'. By this Hazlitt means the fundamental tendency of Wordsworth's reflective verse to refer all experience, of nature and of humanity, to the poet himself. This is a quality which makes Wordsworth's great meditative nature poetry possible, but in its privileging of solitary and subjective conditions over the claims of community, it leads into the second of Hazlitt's objections. This is the unmistakably reactionary outlook and tone of *The Excursion*. The poem frankly rejects all effort towards political change, and Hazlitt is moved to a fine strain of determined radical idealism by one passage in which Wordsworth appears to assert that the radicals have actually suffered justly in the backlash of reaction (presumably because evil institutions are preferable to open and uncertainly directed conflict). Hazlitt's third criticism is that Wordsworth typically idealizes his rustic subjects and offers in his poetry a sentimentally heightened representation of rural life, in the interests of his own attitude to nature. This point anticipates strictures that Coleridge was to make in *Biographia Literaria*.

Hazlitt's famous attack in his lecture 'On the Living Poets' deserves full quotation:

> Mr Wordsworth is at the head of that which has been denominated the Lake school of poetry; a school which, with all my respect for it, I do not think sacred from criticism or exempt from faults, of some of which faults I shall speak with becoming frankness; for I do not see that the liberty of the press ought to be shackled, or freedom of speech curtailed, to screen either its revolutionary or renegado extravagances. This school of poetry had its origins in the French revolution, or rather in those sentiments and opinions which produced that revolution; and which sentiments and opinions were indirectly imported into this country in translations from the German about that period. Our poetical literature . . . wanted something to stir it up, and it found that something in the principles and events of the French revolution. From the impulse it thus received, it rose at once from the most servile imitation and tamest common-place, to the utmost pitch of singularity and paradox. The change in the belles-lettres was as complete, and to many persons as startling, as the change in politics, with which it went hand in hand. There was a mighty ferment in the heads of statesmen and poets, kings and people. According to the prevailing notions, all was to be natural and new. Nothing that was established was to be tolerated. All the common-place figures of poetry . . . were instantly discarded . . . . The object was to reduce all things to an absolute level . . . . The world was to be turned topsy-turvy; and poetry, by the good will of our Adam-wits, was to share its fate and begin *de novo*. It was a time of promise, a renewal of the world and of letters, and the Deucalions, who were to perform this feat of regeneration, were the present poet-laureate [i.e. Southey] and the two authors of the Lyrical Ballads . . . . The paradox they set out with was, that all things are by nature equally fit subjects for poetry; or that if there is any preference to be given, those that are the meanest and most unpromising are the best . . . . They founded the new school on a principle of sheer humanity, on pure nature void of art . . . they were surrounded, in company with the Muses, by a mixed rabble of idle apprentices and Botany Bay convicts, female vagrants, gipsies, meek daughters in the family of Christ, of idiot boys and mad

mothers . . . the distinctions of birth, the vicissitudes of fortune, did not enter into their abstracted, lofty, and levelling calculation of human nature. He who was more than man, with them was none.

The passage is especially valuable for its evocation of the atmosphere in which *Lyrical Ballads* had appeared, and of the revolutionary dimension of the volume which had at that time been taken for granted. There is an acid disillusion in the writing that marks Hazlitt's contempt for Wordsworth's failure to stand by his early ideals. The sarcasm of the last few sentences is stinging in its awareness of just how far from revolutionary intent, in poetry or politics, the poets of the 'Lake School' had now come.

By 1818 Wordsworth had survived the early establishment attack on his style and subject-matter, and had assumed an authoritative reactionary stance in the first instalment (*The Excursion*) of what was intended to form his great epic. In so doing he attracted very strong criticism from his literary heirs. Those who had come under the influence of his early work, such as Hazlitt, now felt betrayed. And younger writers discovered a distressing contradiction between the revolutionary changes Wordsworth had brought about as a young poet, and the establishment figure who was now their own contemporary.

Hazlitt's account of Wordsworth in *The Spirit of the Age* is more measured and sympathetic. Hazlitt now, in 1825, stresses Wordsworth's central importance as the most influential living writer, and he concentrates in this respect on Wordsworth's treatment of nature. Hazlitt again emphasizes the context of Wordsworth's achievement in the revolutionary Europe of the 1790s, but he avoids the bitter, implicitly accusatory manner of his earlier essays. This is partly because Wordsworth has a representative role to play in the larger pattern of Hazlitt's book, which requires a positive and approving tone. But he also fairly acknowledges that Wordsworth was 'the most original poet now living, and the one whose writings could the least be spared'. Wordsworth remains the indispensable Romantic, not simply in the extent of his achievement and influence, but in the inseparability of his poetic career from the changing political atmosphere of the times.

Attacks on Wordsworth from the Tories did not cease once he had alienated the radicals. Hazlitt suggestively contrasts him with Byron in this respect, whose popularity and interest persisted despite his changes of fortune in social terms. Wordsworth never quite satisfied himself that his greatness was established in the public mind. Jeffrey's attacks continued after the publication of *The Excursion*, but the most famous criticisms of the poems and Preface of *Lyrical Ballads* came from his collaborator in that work, Coleridge. In 1817 Coleridge published *Biographia Literaria*, in which he devoted many pages to a sustained critical analysis of the principles underlying Wordsworth's stylistic and thematic innovations in *Lyrical Ballads*. Coleridge's strictures reinforce earlier attacks on these innovations as not simply flawed in logic or credibility, but as implicitly revolutionary assertions of the rights of the common people. Coleridge does not, however, exactly wish to diminish Wordsworth's achievement, but rather to shift attention from the earlier politically dangerous verse, and towards the later reflective and personal poetry. There is something of self-justification in all this. His name had long been associated with Wordsworth's and with *Lyrical Ballads*, but by 1817 he was very far from wishing to be thought of as a fellow-traveller. He too, and in peculiarly neurotic and defensive ways, had a past to live down, and it was necessary to clarify for a potentially hostile reading public what was the true nature of his old friend's achievement.

For Keats and Shelley, and to a lesser extent Byron, Wordsworth was undoubtedly the dominant figure amongst the living and recent poets. Coleridge too exerted considerable influence, but this was of a more strictly literary kind. His handling of blank verse as a medium to express delicate transformations of mood and thought, and the metrical achievements of *The Ancient Mariner* and *Christabel*, proved particularly fruitful innovations of technique. Wordsworth and Coleridge had of course together effected the stylistic revolution of the 1790s, but Wordsworth alone had sustained his poetical career, and had used it publicly to renege on the ideals which had underpinned his innovations in style.

The social responsibility of the poet was a major preoccupation of the young Romantics in the troubled years from 1812 to 1824 (the latter year that of Byron's death). Wordsworth offered above all an exemplary instance of the poet turning away in selfish solitude from his obligations to the community at large, and – so it was construed – opting instead for the comforts and security of orthodoxy.

Shelley and Keats owed their most positive poetic debt to Wordsworth in the treatment of nature. They both inherit a Wordsworthian intimacy of natural description, and they develop Wordsworth's discovery in nature of a repository of forms and images which may serve the representation of subjective consciousness. Their development of this Wordsworthian vision of nature provides their poetry with a sensory basis for the ideal possibilities to which an uncongenial contemporary social experience is contrasted.

All of the three younger Romantics acknowledged quite explicitly their debt to Wordsworth's nature poetry, and to his general stylistic achievement. Shelley's powerful, skilled and funny satire on Wordsworth, *Peter Bell the Third* (written in 1819), includes an eloquent statement on the positive legacy:

> But Peter's verse was clear, and came
>   Announcing from the frozen hearth
> Of a cold age, that none might tame
> The soul of that diviner flame
>   It augured to the Earth:
>
> Like gentle rains, on the dry plains,
>   Making that green which late was grey,
> Or like the sudden moon, that stains
> Some gloomy chamber's window-panes
>   With a broad light like day.
>
> For language was in Peter's hand
>   Like clay, while he was yet a potter;
> And he made songs for all the land
> Sweet both to feel and understand,
>   As pipkins late to mountain Cotter.
>
>   (ll. 433–47)

Shelley's very debt to Wordsworth intensified his disapproval of the older poet's apostasy. In *Alastor* (1816), the earliest of his successful longer works, Shelley tackles the issue. He uses a Wordsworthian figure to narrate the poem, but he also uses the poem's Preface to criticize those who 'attempt to exist without human sympathy'. Such people who 'prepare for their old age a miserable grave' by dooming themselves to 'a slow and poisonous decay' are contrasted with those figures, exemplified in the anonymous poet-protagonist of *Alastor*, who perish in their too-exclusive quest for the ideal. Shelley's poem even takes its epigraph from *The Excursion*, which enforces the personal reference of the Preface and, implicitly, the poem.

Keats's attitude to Wordsworth is less qualified in its indebtedness, just as Keats's relation to his social world is generally less direct in the poetry. In Byron, however, the actual poetic influence is distinctly limited, while the manifest political antipathy is very plain indeed. The positive Wordsworthian influence on Byron is mainly confined to the period of Shelley's first friendship with Byron, in Switzerland during 1816. Its most famous (and most characteristic) expression is in the third Canto of *Childe Harold*, where it sounds an uncertain note, suggesting even perhaps something of a merely faddish pose:

> I live not in myself, but I become
> Portion of that around me; and to me
> High mountains are a feeling, but the hum
> Of human cities torture . . .
>
>   (stanza lxxii)

But when Byron goes on to the offensive in relation to Wordsworth (and the other 'Lakers'), in for example the 'dedication' to *Don Juan*, it is to denigrate Wordsworth's poetic and philosophical pretensions, and to emphasize the older poet's recent acceptance of 'his place in the Excise'.

The second-generation Romantics were nevertheless to discover for themselves just how uncomfortable could be the social alienation that Wordsworth himself had suffered as a young man. For Keats the disapproval of the establishment had directly tragic consequences.

Keats published only three volumes of poetry in his short life. And in a period when literary reviewing wielded its greatest influence, these volumes were singled out for critical abuse of a most distressing and outrageous kind.

It was not the stylistic or thematic qualities of Keats's verse which attracted the notorious attentions of the *Quarterly Review* and *Blackwood's Edinburgh Magazine*. His first volume of poetry did certainly and understandably produce wariness, puzzlement, even derision. In *Endymion* and thereafter, Keats consciously avoided the smooth finished quality of Pope and his followers. His 'primitive' style offended easily (and in a sense deliberately), as an implicit rejection of refinement and an elegant, polished manner; the political resonance of such a challenge to received taste has already been noted in relation to the reception of *Lyrical Ballads*. Keats's odd rhymes could appear laughable, his epithets could appear affected or merely curious. But any serious effort of impartial judgement must have discovered the promise of greatness in Keats's earlier work. No such effort, however, was made by the most powerful commentators. For Keats was a known friend of the radical poet Leigh Hunt, who had promoted the poetry of Keats and Shelley in his weekly paper *The Examiner*. Keats's association with Hunt, and also the apparent poetic influence of Hunt's verse on Keats's work, earned the young poet an extraordinary onslaught from the Tory reviewers.

Hunt was a well-known radical who had actually been imprisoned for remarks he had published about the Prince Regent. As a poet he was labelled by his enemies the leader of the 'Cockney School' of poetry. The name suggested a city-dweller's coarsely sentimental hankering for the rural life as presented in the work of the Lake poets. (Hunt was also much influenced – not, it must be said, entirely for the better – by what he understood to be the doctrines of the Preface to *Lyrical Ballads*.) The term 'Cockney School' also of course hinted at low social origins, contemptible in any man who aspired to write poetry. The attack on Keats was thus grounded in a sneering social superiority that found the combination of poetry and a 'shabby-genteel' ethos both offensively pretentious and pitiably vulgar.

The two most damaging and hurtful attacks on Keats both appeared in 1818. John Gibson Lockhart's review of *Endymion* and the 1817 *Poems* appeared in *Blackwood's* in August, and then in September the *Quarterly's* review was published (though it was dated April). It was generally believed at the time to be the work of Gifford, the editor, though Shelley thought it was the work of Southey. It was in fact by John Wilson Croker. The first part of Lockhart's review seems now barely credible in its tone, and in the criteria of its attack:

> Of all the manias of this mad age, the most incurable, as well as the most common, seems to be no other than the *Metromanie*. The just celebrity of Robert Burns and Miss Baillie has had the melancholy effect of turning the heads of we know not how many farm-servants and unmarried ladies; our very footmen compose tragedies, and there is scarcely a superannuated governess in the island that does not leave a roll of lyrics behind her in her band-box. To witness the disease of any human understanding, however feeble, is distressing; but the spectacle of an able mind reduced to a state of insanity is of course ten times more afflicting. It is with such sorrow as this that we have contemplated the case of Mr John Keats. This young man appears to have received from nature talents of an excellent, perhaps even of a superior order – talents which, devoted to the purposes of any useful profession, must have rendered him a respectable, if not an eminent citizen. His friends, we understand, destined him to the career of medicine, and he was bound apprentice some years ago to a worthy apothecary in town. But all has been undone by a sudden attack of the malady to which we have alluded. Whether Mr John had been sent home with a diuretic or composing draught to some patient far gone in the poetical mania, we have not heard. This much is certain, that he has caught the infection, and that thoroughly. For some time we were in hopes, that he might get off with a violent fit or two; but of late the symptoms are terrible. The phrenzy of the *Poems* was bad enough in its way, but it did not alarm us half so seriously as the calm, settled, imperturbable drivelling idiocy of *Endymion*. We hope, however, that in so young a person, and with a constitution originally so good, even now the disease is not utterly incurable. Time, firm treatment, and rational restraint, do much for many apparently hopeless invalids; and if Mr Keats should happen, at some interval of reason, to cast his eye upon our pages, he may perhaps be convinced of the existence of his malady, which, in such cases, is often all that is necessary to put the patient in a fair way of being cured.

The readers of the *Examiner* newspaper were informed, some

time ago, by a solemn paragraph, in Mr Hunt's best style, of the appearance of two new stars of glorious magnitude and splendour in the poetical horizon of the land of Cockaigne. One of these turned out, by and by, to be no other than Mr John Keats. This precocious adulation confirmed the wavering apprentice in his desire to quit the gallipots, and at the same time excited in his too susceptible mind a fatal admiration for the character and talents of the most worthless and affected of all the versifiers of our time . . . . In [his sonnet to the painter Haydon] Mr Keats classes together WORDSWORTH, HUNT, and HAYDON, as the three greatest spirits of the age, and . . . alludes to himself, and some others of the rising brood of Cockneys, as likely to attain hereafter an equally honourable elevation. Wordsworth and Hunt! what a juxta-position! The purest, the loftiest, and we do not fear to say it, the most classical of living English poets, joined together in the same compliment with the meanest, the filthiest, and the most vulgar of Cockney poetasters . . . [Lockhart continues after quoting from *Endymion*] . . . our youthful poet passes . . . into a long strain of foaming abuse against a certain class of English Poets, whom, with Pope at their head, it is much the fashion with the ignorant unsettled pretenders of the present time to undervalue . . . it is most pitiably ridiculous to hear men, of whom their country will always have reason to be proud, reviled by uneducated and flimsy striplings, who are not capable of understanding either their merits, or those of any other *men of power* – fanciful dreaming tea-drinkers, who, without logic enough to analyse a single idea, or imagination enough to form one original image, or learning enough to distinguish between the written language of Englishmen and the spoken jargon of Cockneys, presume to talk with contempt of some of the most exquisite spirits the world every produced, merely because they did not happen to exert their faculties in laborious affected descriptions of flowers seen in window-pots, or cascades heard at Vauxhall; in short, because they chose to be wits, philosophers, patriots, and poets, rather than to found the Cockney school of versification, morality, and politics, a century before its time.

Lockhart's assault is conducted almost entirely in terms of a social superiority which is underpinned by political antagonism. Keats *was* influenced to a certain extent by Hunt. Hunt's interpretation of the principles of *Lyrical Ballads* led him to produce verse that was certainly mannered and that could be misguidedly prettifying. But Keats's originality, his rapid development beyond the affectation of Hunt towards his own singular and wholly distinctive richness and sensuousness, in reality constitutes the most impressive of the Romantic responses to Wordsworth. For Wordsworth to be held up as a model of unattainable and 'classical' excellence, and contrasted in the most extreme way to Keats, implicitly allied as he is by Lockhart with 'the meanest, the filthiest, and the most vulgar of Cockney poetasters', was a distressing irony indeed.

It was widely believed by contemporaries that Keats's early death was a direct consequence of the vehement Tory attacks in the reviews. Keats was not even the only fatal casualty; John Scott, brilliant editor of the *London Magazine*, was challenged to a duel by Lockhart for his outspoken criticisms of the *Blackwood's* methods, and mortally wounded by Lockhart's deputy. Shelley wrote *Adonais*, his magnificent elegy for Keats, in the conviction that he had effectively been murdered by the Tory reviewers, and he made this plain in his Preface.

It is worth noticing, however, that the connotations of vulgarity and upstart pretension which attached to Keats's poetry also seemed legitimate to Byron. Byron's surprisingly vehement dislike of Keats's work is marked by what one critic has aptly described as a 'socio-sexual revulsion'. The aristocratic Byron shared with his social peers a difficulty in adjusting the received view that theirs was the only social class qualified to write poetry. The difficulty was somehow most acute when the pretension was joined to an immediacy of sensuous experience; this was vulgarity, so to speak, of an especially tasteless sort. Byron's callous joke about Keats in *Don Juan* must be understood in this context:

> John Keats, who was killed off by one critique,
>   Just as he really promised something great,
> If not intelligible, without Greek
>   Contrived to talk about the gods of late,
> Much as they might have been supposed to speak.
>   Poor fellow! His was an untoward fate.
> 'Tis strange the mind, that very fiery particle,
> Should let itself be snuffed out by an article.
>
> (Canto 11, stanza lx)

Of course Keats did not in fact actually die of an illness brought on by reading a review, in the literal sense that Shelley and Byron understood. But Keats, already a very sick man, probably felt that the hostile reviews confirmed the failure and futility of his poetic career, and allowed them to deepen the depression of his last months.

Conclusion

The Romantics worked in a cultural milieu which was powerfully charged with conflicts of political principle and party. A recognition of this fact is fundamental in assessing the nature of the achievement of Blake, Wordsworth and Coleridge, and in evaluating the influence of these first-generation Romantics on the younger poets of the period. The younger Romantics in their turn worked in an atmosphere of great social upheaval, and amidst the threat of actual revolution in England.

Certain basic characteristics of English national life in the decades following the French Revolution are registered in literary terms at the level of stylistic innovation, and in the general orientation of themes in poetry. The struggle of radical idealism with a reactionary establishment is very self-consciously a part of the spirit of the age, and so is the sense of change – as a threat or an optimistic promise – that is to be met with in every sphere of social and cultural experience. The work of the Romantics makes the major contribution to a larger English 'Romanticism' which is widely diverse. This diversity lies in the variety of responses to, and articulations of, a common but constantly changing historical experience. It is this shared participation in an evolving social world, as much as the direct and sometimes personal interactions of influence and debate between poets, which gives the English Romantic movement in poetry its homogeneity.

The deep social engagement of the Romantics' poetry has not been sufficiently emphasized in the critical tradition, and this fact may be related to the challenge that their poetry represents for the industrialized society which was emergent in their own day. They offer areas of experience and response that are potentially subversive, and so the Victorian mediation of their work concentrated on a lyric subjectivity and love of nature which, taken out of their context in the fuller Romantic representation of social experience, constitute a body of Romantic verse which appeared remote from social concerns, and indeed positively in recoil from such concerns. The present century inherited this view, as it inherited too the term 'Romantic' itself.

The word as applied to early nineteenth-century poetry in fact merged two completely distinct meanings. From the second half of the seventeenth century, 'romantic' in English meant a character or action suited to Romance (in the sense of an exotic or far-fetched tale of chivalry in the medieval French manner). 'Romantic' was used in a way rather like its contemporary 'picturesque', to suggest experience more appropriate to make-believe than the real workaday world; 'romantic' referred various areas of experience to the realm of fiction, and 'picturesque' referred certain visual experience to a style of idealized landscape painting.

But 'romantic' had a quite different sense in late eighteenth-century Germany, where it was used to describe a modern school of writers and artists who defined their principles and objectives in opposition to what they saw as a sterile prescriptive classicism. When this rather technical sense was imported into English literary history, its collision with the established English usage gave to English Romanticism an aura of disengaged remoteness from familiar social experience.

The extraordinary immediacy and urgency of the Romantics' social relations call the 'essentialist' definition of the word 'Romantic' into question as a useful critical term. By the 'essentialist' approach is meant that which discerns various timeless and unchanging qualities of experience which are labelled 'Romantic' and which may be encountered in art from any time or place. This approach results in a proliferation of meanings and associations so great that any firm and specific focus on generic qualities of Romanticism is blurred and lost amongst unmanageable variety.

An historical approach avoids this problem, and permits a description and interpretation of Romantic art as the temporally limited production of a particular complex of personalities, social events and developments, at a certain place and time. The manifest continuity of Romantic England with our own society is then not the least important factor making Romantic poetry still accessible and important, in its address to problems and experiences which persist in our present social world.

Chronology

Literary

1757 William Blake b (28 November)
1759 Robert Burns b; Mary Wollstonecraft b
1763 Samuel Rogers b
1770 William Wordsworth b (7 April)
1771 Walter Scott b; Dorothy Wordsworth b
1772 Samuel Taylor Coleridge b (21 October)
1773 Francis Jeffrey b
1774 Robert Southey b; Goethe, *Werther*
1775 Jane Austen b
1776 Edward Gibbon, *Decline and Fall of the Roman Empire*; Tom Paine, *Common Sense*; Adam Smith, *Wealth of Nations*
1777 Thomas Campbell b
1778 William Hazlitt b
1779 Tom Moore b

Historical

1760 George III succeeds to the throne
1768 John Wilkes is expelled from the Commons, and re-elected three times
1774 Louis XVI succeeds to the throne of France
1775 American War of Independence
1776 American Declaration of Independence
1781 British surrender at Yorktown

Literary

1782 Rousseau, *Confessions*

1783 George Crabbe, *The Village*

1784 Leigh Hunt b; Samuel Johnson d

1785 Thomas De Quincey b; Thomas Love Peacock b; William Cowper, *The Task*

1786 Burns, *Poems Chiefly in the Scottish Dialect*

1788 Blake, *No Natural Religion*; George Gordon, Lord Byron b (22 January); Wollstonecraft, *Mary*

1789 Blake, *Book of Thel, Songs of Innocence*; William Lisle Bowles, *Fourteen Sonnets*; Erasmus Darwin, *The Loves of the Plants* (published again in 1791 – but dated 1790 – as pt II of *The Botanic Garden*)

1790 Blake begins *Marriage of Heaven and Hell*; Burke, *Reflections on the Revolution in France*; Wollstonecraft, *Vindication of the Rights of Man*

1791 Boswell, *Life of Johnson*; Cowper's translation of Homer; Darwin, *The Economy of Vegetables* (pt I of *The Botanic Garden*); Paine, *Rights of Man* (pt I)

1792 Shelley b (4 August); Blake, *Marriage of Heaven and Hell*; Paine, *Rights of Man* (pt II); Rogers, *The Pleasures of Memory*; Wollstonecraft,

Historical

1782 Britain negotiates peace with America

1783 First ministry of William Pitt the Younger (b 1759; his first ministry lasts until 1801)

1784 Revolt in the Dutch Netherlands

1787 United States Constitution; revolt in the Austrian Netherlands

1788 Centenary of the 'Glorious Revolution'; George III attacked by an illness (probably porphyria) closely resembling insanity

1789 George III recovers; French 'Third Estate' constitutes itself a National Assembly; French Revolution (storming of the Bastille, 14 July); text of the Declaration of the Rights of Man approved by the French National Assembly (August); rebellion in San Domingo

1791 Anti-Jacobin riots in Birmingham; Louis XVI's abortive 'flight to Varennes' (June); rebellion in Haiti

1792 Pitt attacks the slave trade; Louis XVI imprisoned with his family; 'September Massacres' in Paris; abolition of the monarchy in France;

Literary		Historical	
1792	*Vindication of the Rights of Woman*	1792	War of the First Coalition (to 1797; France declares war on Austria and Prussia in April); invasion of France halted at the Battle of Valmy
1793	John Clare b; Blake, *Visions of the Daughters of Albion, America*; Godwin, *Political Justice*; Wordsworth, *Descriptive Sketches, An Evening Walk*	1793	Louis XVI executed (21 January); England and France declare war (February); Britain, the Netherlands and Spain join the first Coalition; revolt in La Vendée; Marie Antoinette executed (16 October); the 'Terror' in Paris (from September); French 'Girondins' executed (October); treason trials in Scotland; Napoleon crushes independence movement in Corsica
1794	Blake, *Europe, Songs of Innocence and of Experience, Urizen*; Godwin, *Caleb Williams*; Paine, *The Age of Reason* (pt I)	1794	Habeas Corpus suspended (May); State Trials (November; Thomas Holcroft, John Thelwall, Horne Tooke and others acquitted of treason); Robespierre executed (July)
1795	Keats b (31 October); Boswell d; Blake, *Book of Ahania, Book of Los, Song of Los*; Paine, *The Age of Reason* (pt II)	1795	'Two Acts' passed (against seditious meetings and treasonable practices)
1796	Burke, *Letters on a Regicide Peace*; Burns d; Coleridge, *Poems on Various Subjects, The Watchman* (political newspaper in ten numbers); Darwin, *Zoonomia*; Southey, *Joan of Arc*; Wollstonecraft, *Letters Written . . . in Sweden, Norway and Denmark*	1796	Threat of French invasion
1797	Blake begins *Vala* (later renamed *The Four Zoas*); Coleridge writes 'Kubla Khan'; Godwin and Wollstonecraft married; Mary Wollstonecraft Godwin b (marries Shelley, 1816); Wollstonecraft d;	1797	Two serious naval mutinies (at Spithead and the Nore, April to June); Whigs secede from attendance in parliament; peace treaty between France and Austria; republics established in Venice, Genoa and Milan

Literary

Historical

1797 Wordsworth completes first version of *The Ruined Cottage*; close friendship between Wordsworth and Coleridge in Somerset; *The Anti-Jacobin*

1798 Coleridge, *Fears in Solitude, France, an Ode, Frost at Midnight*; Godwin, *Memoir of Mary Wollstonecraft*; Walter Savage Landor, *Gebir*; Thomas Malthus, *Essay on the Principle of Population*; Wollstonecraft, *Posthumous Works*; Wordsworth and Coleridge, *Lyrical Ballads* (includes Wordsworth, 'Tintern Abbey', and Coleridge, *The Ancient Mariner*); Wordsworth plans scheme for *The Recluse*

1799 Campbell, *The Pleasures of Hope*; Wordsworth completes first version of *The Prelude*

1798 Rebellion in Ireland; Nelson destroys the French fleet in the battle of the Nile; Helvetic and Roman republics proclaimed; War of the Second Coalition (to 1801); Pitt forges alliance against France of Britain, Russia, Austria, Naples, Portugal and Turkey

1799 Legal and political suppression of radicals in Britain; Napoleon becomes First Consul after the *coup* of eighteenth Brumaire

1800 Act of Union with Ireland (February); Fox returns to parliament; Battle of Marengo (June); Malta falls to English

1801 Southey, *Thalaba*; Wordsworth and Coleridge, 2nd, two-volume edition of *Lyrical Ballads* (dated 1800), with Preface

1801 Pitt, Windham and Grenville resign over Catholic emancipation (it is resisted by George III); Addington's ministry (lasts until 1804); Nelson destroys Danish fleet at Copenhagen

1802 *Edinburgh Review* founded; Scott, *Minstrelsy of the Scottish Border*; Cobbett's *Weekly Political Register* founded; Wordsworth and Coleridge, 3rd edition of *Lyrical Ballads* with extended Preface; Wordsworth begins 'Immortality Ode' (completed 1804), and works on a longer version of *The Prelude* (completed 1805)

1802 Peace of Amiens (March) halts hostilities between England and France for 14 months; Napoleon is made life consul; French army enters Switzerland

Literary

Historical

		1803	Declaration of war with France (May); Robert Emmet executed in Ireland
1804	Blake working on *Milton* and *Jerusalem*	1804	Renewed mental illness of George III; Addington's ministry collapses; Pitt forms his second ministry (lasts until 1806); Napoleon is made emperor; introduction in France of the *Code Napoléon*; Britain at war with Spain (December)
1805	Scott, *Lay of the Last Minstrel*; Southey, *Madoc*	1805	War of the Third Coalition against France (to 1807; Pitt negotiates alliance with Russia, then Austria); Napoleon crowned king of Italy; Napoleon wins important victories in the Battles of Ulm (October) and Austerlitz (November); Nelson dies from wounds received during his naval victory at Trafalgar (October)
		1806	Prussia joins Third Coalition; Pitt d; 'Ministry of all the Talents', Grenville Prime Minister; Charles James Fox d (b 1749)
1807	Byron, *Hours of Idleness*; Moore, *Irish Melodies*; Southey, *Letters from England*; Wordsworth, *Poems in Two Volumes*	1807	Grenville resigns over Catholic emancipation; Portland Prime Minister; slave trade abolished (25 March); British fleet bombards Copenhagen; Peninsular War begins
1808	Scott, *Marmion*	1808	Joseph Bonaparte becomes King of Spain; Convention of Cintra (August)
1809	*Quarterly Review* founded; Byron, *English Bards and Scotch Reviewers*; Campbell, *Gertrude of Wyoming*; Coleridge, *The Friend* (28 numbers; concludes 1810); Wordsworth, *Convention of Cintra*	1809	Death of Sir John Moore in the Battle of Corunna (January); Napoleon captures Vienna, and is excommunicated; Pope Pius VII imprisoned; Walcheren expedition fails; Portland resigns; Perceval Prime Minister

Literary

1810 Blake completes work on *Milton* (probably); Crabbe, *The Borough*; Scott, *The Lady of the Lake*; Southey, *The Curse of Kehama*

1811 Austen, *Sense and Sensibility*

1812 Byron, speeches in the Lords on Luddites and on Catholic Emancipation, and publishes *Childe Harold's Pilgrimage* (Cantos I and II); Crabbe, *Tales*; James and Horace Smith, *Rejected Addresses*

1813 Scott refuses laureateship; Southey becomes Poet Laureate; Austen, *Pride and Prejudice*; Byron, *The Bride of Abydos*, *The Giaour*; Scott, *Rokeby*; Shelley, *Queen Mab*; Southey, *Life of Nelson*

1814 Austen, *Mansfield Park*; Byron, *The Corsair*, *Lara*; Hunt, *The Feast of the Poets*; Southey, *Roderick*; Wordsworth, *The Excursion*

1815 Byron, *Hebrew Melodies*; Hunt, *The Descent of Liberty*; Wordsworth, *Poems* (first collected edition, with important preface)

Historical

1810 Introduction of first reform bill since 1797; Napoleon annexes Holland; general acceptance of George III's 'insanity' (December)

1811 Prince of Wales becomes Prince Regent (5 February); 'Luddite' insurgency in the Midlands (from November)

1812 Perceval assassinated in the House of Commons (11 May); Lord Liverpool forms a government; Castlereagh becomes Foreign Secretary; British gains in the Peninsular War; Britain at war with America; Napoleon invades Russia (June); Napoleon retreats from Moscow with heavy losses (October to December)

1813 Failed Peace Congress in Prague; Wellington wins significant success in the Peninsular War; Switzerland, Holland, Italy, Spain and other states are liberated from French rule; Leigh Hunt imprisoned (until 1815) for libelling the Prince Regent; War of the Fourth Coalition (to 1814); Castlereagh negotiates agreements with Russia, Prussia, Sweden, Austria and German States.

1814 France invaded by allies of the Fourth Coalition (1 January); Paris falls (March); Napoleon abdicates (April), and is exiled to Elba (May); Bourbon monarchy restored; peace between Britain and America; Congress of Vienna (September, until June 1815)

1815 Napoleon escapes from Elba and returns to France (the 'Hundred Days', March to June); allied armies defeat the French at Waterloo (18 June);

Literary

Historical

		1815	Napoleon surrenders (15 July), and is exiled to St Helena; Louis XVIII restored to the French throne
1816	Austen, *Emma*; Byron, *Childe Harold's Pilgrimage* (Canto III), *The Siege of Corinth*, *Parisina*, *The Prisoner of Chillon*; Coleridge, *Christabel, Kubla Khan, and The Pains of Sleep*, *The Statesman's Manual*; Hunt, *The Story of Rimini*; Hunt's 'Young Poets' article in the *Examiner*; Shelley, *Alastor… and Other Poems*; Wordsworth carries out major revisions to *The Prelude* (to 1819); Shelley and Byron meet in Switzerland (June and July); Shelley and Keats become acquainted through friendship with Leigh Hunt (from December)	1816	Post-war depression; Spa Fields riot (2 December)
1817	Austen d; *Blackwood's Edinburgh Magazine* ('*Maga*') founded; Byron, *Manfred*, *The Lament of Tasso*; Coleridge, *A Lay Sermon, Biographia Literaria, Sibylline Leaves*; Hazlitt, *Characters of Shakespeare's Plays*, *The Round Table*; Keats, *Poems*; Moore, *Lalla Rookh*; Shelley, *Laon and Cythna* (reissued and revised in 1818 as *The Revolt of Islam*)	1817	Habeas corpus suspended (4 March); legal suppression of democratic societies; Prince Regent's daughter, Princess Charlotte d; British government purchases the Elgin Marbles for the British Museum
1818	Austen, *Northanger Abbey*, *Persuasion*; Byron, *Childe Harold's Pilgrimage* (Canto IV), *Beppo*; Hazlitt, *Lectures on the English Poets*; Hunt, *Foliage*; Keats, *Endymion*; Croker's attack on Keats in the *Quarterly Review*; Lockhart's attack on Keats in *Blackwood's Edinburgh Magazine*; Mary Shelley, *Frankenstein*	1818	Habeas Corpus restored (never subsequently suspended); Castlereagh attends conference of European Alliance; motion in parliament for universal suffrage (defeated)

Literary

1819 Byron, *Mazeppa, Don Juan* (Cantos I and II); Crabbe, *Tales of the Hall*; Hazlitt, *Lectures on the English Comic Writers*; Shelley, *Rosalind and Helen . . . with Other Poems*, writes *The Mask of Anarchy* (not published until 1832); Wordsworth, *Peter Bell, The Waggoner*

1820 *London Magazine* founded; Blake finishes first complete copy of *Jerusalem*; Clare, *Poems Descriptive of Rural Life and Scenery*; Keats, *Lamia, Isabella, The Eve of St Agnes, and other Poems*; Shelley, *The Cenci, Prometheus Unbound . . . with Other Poems, Swellfoot the Tyrant* (suppressed on publication)

1821 Keats d (23 February); Byron, *Marino Faliero, Sardanapalus, The Two Foscari, Cain, Don Juan* (Cantos III–V); Clare, *The Village Minstrel*; De Quincey, *Confessions of an English Opium Eater*; Hazlitt, *Table Talk* (concluded 1822); Shelley, *Adonais, Epipsychidion*, writes 'A Defence of Poetry' (not published until 1840); Southey, *A Vision of Judgment*

1822 Shelley working on *The Triumph of Life* (published in 1824); Shelley d (8 July); Byron, *The Vision of Judgment* (published in *The Liberal*), *Werner*; Shelley, *Hellas*

1823 Byron, *Don Juan* (Cantos VI–XIV), *Heaven and Earth* (in *The Liberal*); Lamb, *Essays of Elia* (first series)

1824 Byron d (19 April); Byron, *Don Juan* (Cantos XV–XVI), *The Deformed Transformed*; Shelley, *Posthumous Poems*

Historical

1819 Peterloo Massacre (16 August); passing in parliament of the 'Six Acts', powerful measures for the suppression of meetings and activities

1820 Revolution in Spain (January) and Naples (July). George III d; accession of George IV; the 'Cato Street Conspiracy' discovered; trial of George IV's wife, Queen Caroline; European Conference to co-ordinate measures against European movements for revolution

1821 Napoleon d; Queen Caroline d; Greek War of Independence (begins in March); defeat of uprising in Naples; motion for parliamentary reform defeated

1822 Castlereagh d (suicide)

Literary	Historical
1825 Coleridge, *Aids to Reflection*; Hazlitt, *The Spirit of the Age*	*No further entries*
1826 Hazlitt, *The Plain Speaker*	
1827 Blake d (12 August); Clare, *The Shepherd's Calendar*	
1829 Coleridge, *On the Constitution of the Church and State*	
1830 Hazlitt d	
1832 Crabbe d; Scott d	
1833 Lamb, *Last Essays of Elia*	
1834 Coleridge d (25 July); Lamb d	
1835 Clare, *The Rural Muse*	
1843 Southey d; Wordsworth becomes Poet Laureate	
1850 Wordsworth d (23 April); Wordsworth, *The Prelude* (so titled by his widow Mary)	
1864 Clare d	

Bibliography

The historical context
Good and interesting general histories include the following:

Asa Briggs, *The Age of Improvement* (1959)
Ian R. Christie, *Wars and Revolutions* (1982)
Elie Halévy, *England in 1815* (1913; trans. E. I. Watkin and D. A. Barker, 1924)
John B. Owen, *The Eighteenth Century, 1714–1815* (1974)
J. Steven Watson, *The Reign of George III, 1760–1815* (1960)
E. L. Woodward, *The Age of Reform, 1815–1870* (1938)
See also the *New Cambridge Modern History*, volume VIII, *The American and French Revolutions, 1763–93* (1965), and volume IX, *War and Peace in an Age of Upheaval, 1793–1830* (1965).

There are many fine and richly detailed biographies of major political figures in the period which also give a more general account of events and atmosphere, including:

C. J. Bartlett, *Castlereagh* (1966)
John Brooke, *King George III* (1972)
John Derry, *Charles James Fox* (1972)
Denis Gray, *Spencer Perceval, 1762–1812: The Evangelical Prime Minister* (1963)
Christopher Hibbert, *George IV* (1976)
Leslie Mitchell, *Holland House* (1980)
John Holland Rose, *William Pitt and the Great War* (1911)
Philip Ziegler, *Addington: A Life of Henry Addington, First Viscount Sidmouth* (1965)

On demographic, economic and agrarian issues, see:

T. S. Ashton, *The Industrial Revolution* (1948)
J. D. Chambers and G. E. Mingay, *The Agricultural Revolution, 1750–1880* (1966)
M. W. Flinn, *British Population Growth, 1700–1850* (1970)
E. L. Jones and G. E. Mingay (eds), *Land, Labour and Population in the Industrial Revolution* (1967)

Peter Mathias, *The First Industrial Nation: an Economic History of Britain, 1700–1914* (1914)
G. E. Mingay, *The Gentry* (1976)

There is a huge body of commentary on political and socio-economic reactions to the French Revolution, including the consequent development of British political radicalism and radical literary culture, and the progress of the protracted European wars fought in the revolutionary and Napoleonic periods; the following is merely a selection:

P. A. Brown, *The French Revolution in English History* (1918)
Marilyn Butler (ed.), *Burke, Paine, Godwin, and the Revolution Controversy* (1984)
A. Cobban (ed.), *The Debate on the French Revolution* (2nd edn, 1950)
Carl B. Cone, *The English Jacobins: Reformers in Late Eighteenth-Century England* (1968)
F. O. Darvall, *Popular Disturbances and Public Order in Regency England* (2nd edn, 1969)
Clive Emsley, *British Society and the French Wars, 1793–1815* (1979)
Albert Goodwin, *The Friends of Liberty: The English Democratic Movement in the Age of the French Revolution* (1979)
J. F. C. Harrison, *The Second Coming* (1979)
J. Anne Hone, *For the Cause of Truth: Radicalism in London, 1796–1821* (1982)
A. Lincoln, *Some Political and Social Ideas of English Dissent, 1763–1800* (1938)
Iain McCalman, *Radical Underworld: Prophets, Revolutionaries and Pornographers in London, 1795–1840* (1988)
S. Maccoby, *English Radicalism, 1786–1832* (1955)
Frank O'Gorman, *The Whig Party and the French Revolution* (1967)
Harold Perkin, *The Origins of Modern English Society, 1780–1880* (1969)
D. Read, *Peterloo: The 'Massacre' and its Background* (1973)
J. M. Roberts, *The Mythology of the Secret Societies* (1972)
R. B. Rose, 'The Priestley riots of 1791', *Past and Present*, 18 (1960)
M. I. Thomis, *The Luddites* (1970)
E. P. Thompson, *The Making of the English Working Class* (rev. edn, 1968)
G. S. Veitch, *The Genesis of Parliamentary Reform* (2nd edn, 1965)
G. A. Williams, *Artisans and Sans Culottes* (1968)

On France and the European context:

Vincent Cronin, *Napoleon* (1971)
Franklin L. Ford, *Europe 1780–1830* (1970)
Albert Goodwin, *The French Revolution* (1953)
E. J. Hobsbawm, *The Age of Revolution, 1789–1848* (1962)
Georges Lefebvre, *The French Revolution* (2 vols, trans. 1962, 1964)
J. M. Roberts, *The French Revolution* (1978)
George Rudé, *Revolutionary Europe, 1783–1815* (1964)
Simon Schama, *Citizens: A Chronicle of the French Revolution* (1989)
A. Soboul, *The French Revolution, 1787–1799* (trans. 1975)
D. M. G. Sutherland, *France 1789–1815: Revolution and Counterrevolution* (1985)

The literary culture of the English Romantics
M. H. Abrams, *The Mirror and the Lamp* (1953)

——, *Natural Supernaturalism* (1971)
David Aers, Jon Cook and David Punter, *Romanticism and Ideology: Studies in English Writing 1765–1830* (1981)
R. D. Altick, *The English Common Reader: A Social History of the Mass Reading Public, 1800–1900* (1957)
A. Aspinall, *Politics and the Press, c. 1780–1850* (1949)
F. Barker *et al.* (eds), *1789: Reading Writing Revolution* (1982)
James Boulton, *The Language of Politics in the Age of Wilkes and Burke* (1963)
C. P. Brand, *Italy and the English Romantics* (1957)
Marilyn Butler, *Jane Austen and the War of Ideas* (1975)
——, *Peacock Displayed: A Satirist in his Context* (1979)
——, *Romantics, Rebels and Reactionaries: English Literature and its Background, 1760–1830* (1981)
Geoffrey Carnall, *Robert Southey and his Age* (1960)
Colin Clair, *A History of Printing in Britain* (1965)
John Clive, *Scotch Reviewers: The 'Edinburgh Review,' 1802–1815* (1957)
Amy Cruse, *The Englishman and his Books in the Early Nineteenth Century* (1930)
James Engell, *The Creative Imagination: Enlightenment to Romanticism* (1981)
Philip Gaskell, *A New Introduction to Bibliography* (corrected edn, 1974)
M. Dorothy George, *English Political Caricature: A Study of Opinion and Propaganda, 1793–1832* (1959)
John Gross, *The Rise and Fall of the Man of Letters* (1969)
Hugh Honour, *Romanticism* (1982)
John O. Hayden, *Romantic Bards and Scotch Reviewers* (1971)
Draper Hill, *Fashionable Contrasts* (1966)
——, *Mr Gillray the Caricaturist* (1965)
Ian Jack, *Oxford History of English Literature, 1815–1832* (1963)
Gary Kelly, *The English Jacobin Novel, 1780–1805* (1976)
Jon P. Klancher, *The Making of English Reading Audiences, 1790–1832* (1987)
Jerome J. McGann, *The Beauty of Inflections* (1985)
——, *The Romantic Ideology: A Critical Investigation* (1983)
F. A. Mumby, *Publishing and Bookselling* (1974)
H. W. Piper, *The Active Universe* (1962)
Marjorie Plant, *The English Book Trade: An Economic History of the Making and Sale of Books* (1939)
D. H. Reiman (ed.), *The Romantics Reviewed* (9 vols, 1972)
W. L. Renwick, *Oxford History of English Literature, 1789–1815* (1963)
Derek Roper, *Reviewing Before the 'Edinburgh', 1788–1802* (1978)
William St Clair, *The Godwins and the Shelleys* (1989)
R. E. Schofield, *The Lunar Society of Birmingham* (1963)
Olivia Smith, *The Politics of Language, 1790–1818* (1984)
Claire Tomalin, *The Life and Death of Mary Wollstonecraft* (1974)
Gerald P. Tyson, *Joseph Johnson: A Liberal Publisher* (1979)
R. K. Webb, *The British Working-Class Reader, 1790–1848* (1955)
William Wickwar, *The Struggle for the Freedom of the Press, 1819–1832* (1928)
Raymond Williams, *The Country and the City* (1973)
——, *Culture and Society, 1780–1950* (1958)
——, *The Long Revolution* (1966)
Carl Woodring, *Politics in English Romantic Poetry* (1972)

The English Romantic poets

Wordsworth

Texts

The standard edition of Wordsworth's poetry has for the past half-century been the *Poetical Works*, ed. E. de Selincourt and Helen Darbishire (Oxford, 1940–9), but this edition is now being superseded by the Cornell Wordsworth. Volumes so far published in this series are:
The Salisbury Plain Poems, ed. Stephen Gill (Ithaca, 1975)
The Prelude, 1798–99, ed. Stephen Parrish (Ithaca, 1977)
Home at Grasmere, ed. Beth Darlington (Ithaca, 1977)
The Ruined Cottage and The Pedlar, ed. James Butler (Ithaca, 1979)
Benjamin the Waggoner, ed. Paul F. Betz (Ithaca, 1981)
The Borderers, ed. Robert Osborn (Ithaca, 1982)
Poems in Two Volumes, ed. Jared R. Curtis (Ithaca, 1983)
An Evening Walk, ed. James Averill (Ithaca, 1984)
Descriptive Sketches, ed. Eric Birdsall (Ithaca, 1984)
Peter Bell, ed. John E. Jordan (Ithaca, 1985)
The Fourteen-Book Prelude, ed. W. J. B. Owen (Ithaca, 1985)
The Tuft of Primroses With Other Late Poems for the Recluse, ed. Joseph Kishel (Ithaca, 1986)
The White Doe of Rylstone, ed. Kristine Dugas (Ithaca, 1988)
Shorter Poems 1807–1820, ed. Carl H. Ketcham (Ithaca, 1989)

The best single-volume text of the poetry is the Oxford Authors *William Wordsworth*, ed. Stephen Gill (Oxford, 1984). Also very useful are the Norton Critical Edition text of *The Prelude 1799, 1805, 1850*, eds Jonathan Wordsworth, M. H. Abrams and Stephen Gill (1979); *Lyrical Ballads 1798*, ed. W. J. B. Owen (1974); and *Lyrical Ballads 1805*, ed. Derek Roper (1968). The most compact and affordable relatively complete text is the Penguin *Poems* edited in two volumes by John O. Hayden, but users should consult the Introduction to Hayden's text for a clear understanding of the edition's scope and purposes.

The standard edition of the prose is *The Prose Works*, eds W. J. B. Owen and Jane Worthington Smyser (3 vols, Oxford, 1974). The letters are best consulted in *Letters of William and Dorothy Wordsworth*, ed. E. de Selincourt (Oxford); *The Early Years, 1787–1805*, revised Chester L. Shaver (Oxford, 1967); *The Middle Years, 1806–11*, revised Mary Moorman (Oxford, 1969); *The Middle Years, 1812–20*, revised Mary Moorman and Alan G. Hill (Oxford, 1970); *The Later Years, 1821–50*, revised Alan G. Hill (Oxford, 1978–   ). See also William and Mary Wordsworth, *The Love Letters*, ed. Beth Darlington (Ithaca, 1981).

An important source is the *Journals of Dorothy Wordsworth*, ed. Mary Moorman. Mark L. Reed's *Wordsworth: the Chronology of the Early Years 1770–1799* (Cambridge, Mass., 1967), and *Middle Years 1800–1815* (Cambridge, Mass., 1975), are invaluable.

The best modern biography is by Stephen Gill, *William Wordsworth* (1989).

Criticism

M. H. Abrams (ed.), *Wordsworth: A Collection of Critical Essays* (1972)
James K. Chandler, *Wordsworth's Second Nature: A Study of the Poetry and Politics* (1984)
C. C. Clarke, *Romantic Paradox* (1962)
Jared R. Curtis, *Wordsworth's Experiments with Tradition: The Lyric Poems of 1802* (1971)
Heather Glen, *Vision and Disenchantment: Blake's 'Songs' and Wordsworth's 'Lyrical Ballads'* (1983)
Paul Hamilton, *Wordsworth* (1986)
Geoffrey H. Hartman, *Wordsworth's Poetry 1787–1814* (1964)
Mary Jacobus, *Tradition and Experiment in Wordsworth's Lyrical Ballads* (1976)
Kenneth R. Johnston, *Wordsworth and the Recluse* (1984)
Marjorie Levinson, *Wordsworth's Great Period Poems* (1986)
Herbert Lindenberger, *On Wordsworth's Prelude* (1963)
Graham McMaster (ed.), *William Wordsworth* (1972)
Stephen Maxfield Parrish, *The Art of the Lyrical Ballads* (1973)
R. Onorato, *The Character of the Poet* (1971)
Nicholas Roe, *Wordsworth and Coleridge: The Radical Years* (1988)
Christopher Salvesen, *The Landscape of Memory* (1965)
Paul Sheats, *The Making of Wordsworth's Poetry 1785–98* (1973)
David Simpson, *Wordsworth and the Figuring of the Real* (1982)
——, *Wordsworth's Historical Imagination* (1987)
John Williams, *Wordsworth: Romantic Poetry and Revolution Politics* (1989)
Jonathan Wordsworth (ed.), *Bicentenary Wordsworth Studies* (1970)
——, *The Music of Humanity* (1969)
——, *William Wordsworth: The Borders of Vision* (1982)

Coleridge

Texts

There is no modern edition of Coleridge's poetical works. The *Complete Poetical Works*, ed. E. H. Coleridge (2 vols, Oxford, 1912), therefore remains the only relatively thorough edition, but it is long out of date. The Everyman text edited by John Beer (1963) provides a useful reading edition for the poetry, but the best working text is now the Oxford Authors *Samuel Taylor Coleridge*, ed. H. J. Jackson (Oxford, 1985), which includes all of the important poetry and a generous selection from the prose. Coleridge's prose writings, across a bewildering variety of forms, amount to a huge body of material, which is gradually receiving the careful editorial work it deserves and requires in the monumental *Collected Coleridge* published by Princeton University Press and Routledge. Volumes which have appeared to date are:

Lectures 1795: On Politics and Religion, eds Lewis Patton and Peter Mann (Princeton, 1971)
The Watchman, ed. Lewis Patton (Princeton, 1970)
Essays on his Times, ed. D. V. Erdman (3 vols, Princeton, 1978)
The Friend, ed. B. Rooke (2 vols, Princeton, 1969)
Lay Sermons, ed. R. J. White (Princeton, 1972)

Biographia Literaria, eds Walter J. Bate and James Engell (2 vols, Princeton, 1983)
On the Constitution of the Church and State, ed. John Colmer (Princeton, 1976)
Marginalia, ed. George Whalley (5 vols, vol. 1, Princeton, 1980, vol. 2, Princeton, 1984)
Logic, ed. J. R. de J. Jackson (Princeton, 1981)

There are two further very important scholarly editions of writings by Coleridge. These are the *Notebooks*, edited to date in three double volumes (of a projected five) by Kathleen Coburn (1957–   ), and the *Letters* edited in six volumes by E. L. Griggs (Oxford, 1956–71).

There is a marvellously sympathetic and readable biography by Richard Holmes, *Coleridge: Early Visions* (1989), covering the earlier years; a concluding second volume is under preparation. Also interesting is Walter Jackson Bate, *Coleridge* (1968).

Criticism

J. A. Appleyard, *Coleridge's Philosophy of Literature: The Development of a Concept of Poetry 1791–1819* (1965)
John Beer, *Coleridge the Visionary* (1959)
——, *Coleridge's Poetic Intelligence* (1977)
——, (ed.), *Coleridge's Variety: Bicentenary Studies* (1974)
Kathleen Coburn (ed.), *Coleridge: A Collection of Critical Essays* (1967)
John Colmer, *Coleridge: Critic of Society* (1959)
Jerome Christensen, *Coleridge's Blessed Machine of Language* (1981)
Kelvin Everest, *Coleridge's Secret Ministry: The Context of the Conversation Poems, 1795–1798* (1979)
Richard H. Fogle, *The Idea of Coleridge's Criticism* (1959)
Norman Fruman, *Coleridge the Damaged Archangel* (1971)
Paul Hamilton, *Coleridge's Poetics* (1983)
Humphrey House, *Coleridge* (1953)
Nigel Leask, *The Politics of Imagination in Coleridge's Critical Thought* (1988)
Thomas McFarland, *Coleridge and the Pantheist Tradition* (1969)
Lucy Newlyn, *Coleridge, Wordsworth, and the Language of Allusion* (1986)
Nicholas Roe, *Wordsworth and Coleridge: The Radical Years* (1988)
Elisabeth Schneider, *Coleridge, Opium and 'Kubla Khan'* (1953)
Elinor Schaffer, *'Kubla Khan' and The Fall of Jerusalem* (1975)
George Watson, *Coleridge the Poet* (1966)
K. M. Wheeler, *The Creative Mind in Coleridge's Poetry* (1981)
Carl Woodring, *Politics in the Poetry of Coleridge* (1961)
Ian Wylie, *Young Coleridge and the Philosophers of Nature* (1989)

Blake

Texts

Blake's poetry should be read wherever possible in a form giving some idea of its 'illuminated' original presentation. This is however by no means easy, so an annotated text giving information about decorative and illustrated features is usually a practicable alternative. *The Illuminated Blake*, ed. David Erdman (rev.

edn, Oxford, 1975) is complete, but in black-and-white and with a sometimes eccentric commentary. There are very good facsimile editions of individual works, however, which are strongly recommended, notably *Songs of Innocence and of Experience*, ed. Sir Geoffrey Keynes (Oxford, 1970), and *The Marriage of Heaven and Hell*, ed. Sir Geoffrey Keynes (Oxford, 1971). The Longman 'Annotated English Poets' text *Blake: The Complete Poems*, ed. W. H. Stevenson with a text by David Erdman, has useful notes but, even in its revised form (London, 1989) the commentary is very uneven, there are no illustrations, and the text is somewhat unreliable. Other very useful but unillustrated texts include *The Complete Writings of William Blake*, ed. Sir Geoffrey Keynes (rev. edn, 1966), the Penguin *Complete Poems of William Blake*, ed. Alicia Ostriker (1977), and *The Prose and Poetry of William Blake*, ed. David Erdman (New York, 1965).

Other important primary texts are the *Letters*, ed. Sir Geoffrey Keynes (1956), and the *Notebook*, ed. David Erdman (Oxford, 1973). There is no satisfactory modern biography of Blake. Much information will be found in the lives by A. Gilchrist (1863; rev. edn by R. Todd, 1945) and Kathleen Raine (1970).

Criticism

Donald Ault, *Visionary Physics: Blake's Response to Newton* (1974)
John Beer, *Blake's Humanism* (1968)
Bernard Blackstone, *English Blake* (1949)
Harold Bloom, *Blake's Apocalypse: A Study in Poetic Argument* (1963)
Jacob Bronowski, *William Blake: A Man without a Mask* (1944; reissued 1965 as *William Blake and the Age of Revolution*)
Stuart Curran and J. A. Wittreich Jr (eds), *Blake's Sublime Allegory* (1973)
S. Foster Damon, *A Blake Dictionary: The Ideas and Symbols of William Blake* (1965)
——, *William Blake: His Philosophy and Symbols* (1924)
David V. Erdman, *Blake: Prophet Against Empire* (3rd rev. edn, 1977)
—— and John E. Grant (eds), *Blake's Visionary Forms Dramatic* (1970)
Northrop Frye, *Fearful Symmetry: A Study of William Blake* (1947)
Robert F. Gleckner, *The Piper and the Bard: A Study of William Blake* (1959)
Heather Glen, *Vision and Disenchantment: Blake's 'Songs' and Wordsworth's 'Lyrical Ballads'* (1983)
E. D. Hirsch, *Innocence and Experience: An Introduction to Blake* (1964)
Edward Larrissy, *William Blake* (1985)
Zachary Leader, *Reading Blake's Songs* (1981)
Anne Mellor, *Blake's Human Form Divine* (1974)
W. J. T. Mitchell, *Blake's Composite Art* (1978)
Morton Paley, *Energy and Imagination: A Study of the Development of Blake's Thought* (1970)
—— and Michael Philips (eds), *William Blake: Essays in Honour of Sir Geoffrey Keynes* (1973)
Michael Philips (ed.), *Interpreting Blake* (1978)
Kathleen Raine, *Blake and Tradition* (1969)
——, *William Blake* (1971)

Byron

Texts

The standard edition of Byron's poetry is the *Complete Poetical Works*, ed. Jerome J. McGann, (7 vols, Oxford, 1980-9). The best reading text is the Oxford Authors *Lord Byron*, ed. Jerome J. McGann (Oxford, 1986). For Byron's other writings, see *Byron's Letters and Journals*, ed. Leslie Marchand, (12 vols, 1973-81). There is a wealth of valuable material in the *Works of Lord Byron, Poetry*, ed. E. H. Coleridge, (7 vols, 1898-1904) and the *Works of Lord Byron. Letters and Journals*, ed. R. E. Prothero, (6 vols, 1898-1901).

The standard life is Leslie A. Marchand, *Byron, A Biography*, (3 vols, 1958), with a one-volume version aimed at the more general reader, *Byron. A Portrait* (1971)

Criticism

Bernard Beatty, *Byron's Don Juan* (1985)
—— and Vincent Newey (eds), *Byron and the Limits of Fiction* (1988)
Elizabeth Boyd, *Byron's 'Don Juan'* (1945)
Michael Cooke, *The Blind Man Traces the Circle* (1969)
Louis Crompton, *Byron and Greek Love* (1985)
Francis Doherty, *Byron* (1968)
Michael Foot, *The Politics of Paradise* (1988)
Robert F. Gleckner, *Byron and the Ruins of Paradise* (1967)
M. K. Joseph, *Byron the Poet* (1964)
John D. Jump, *Byron: A Symposium* (1975)
Malcolm Kelsall, *Byron's Politics* (1987)
Jerome J. McGann, *Don Juan in Context* (1976)
—— , *Fiery Dust: Byron's Poetic Development* (1968)
Peter Manning, *Byron and his Fictions* (1978)
Leslie Marchand, *Byron's Poetry* (1965)
Philip Martin, *Byron: A Poet Before his Public* (1982)
Andrew Rutherford, *Byron: A Critical Study* (1961)
Mark Storey, *Byron and the Eye of Appetite* (1986)
P. West, *Byron and the Spoiler's Art* (1960)

Keats

Texts

There is an excellent modern scholarly edition of the poetry, *The Poems of John Keats*, ed. Jack Stillinger (1978); this edition should be consulted in conjunction with Stillinger's *The Texts of Keats's Poems* (Cambridge, Mass., 1974). The Longman 'Annotated English Poets' *Poems of John Keats*, ed. Miriam Allott (1970) has very full and interesting notes. The Penguin *Complete Poems*, ed. John Barnard (1973) is also very reliable and thorough. The standard edition of Keats's letters is *The Letters of John Keats: 1814-1821*, ed. Hyder Rollins (2 vols, Cambridge, Mass., 1958); *The Letters of John Keats*, ed. Robert Gittings (1970) offers a valuable selection. There is a particularly good volume on Keats in the 'Critical Heritage' series, *Keats: The Critical Heritage*, ed. G. M. Matthews (1971).

There are three good biographies of Keats: Walter Jackson Bate, *John Keats* (1964), Robert Gittings, *John Keats* (1968), and Aileen Ward, *John Keats: The Making of a Poet* (1963).

Criticism

Jeffrey Baker, *John Keats and Symbolism* (1986)
John Barnard, *John Keats* (1987)
Morris Dickstein, *Keats and his Poetry: A Study in Development* (1971)
Claude L. Finney, *The Evolution of Keats's Poetry* (1936)
R. H. Fogle, *The Imagery of Keats and Shelley: A Comparative Study* (1949)
G. S. Fraser (ed.), *John Keats: Odes* (corrected edn, 1985)
Ian Jack, *Keats and the Mirror of Art* (1967)
John Jones, *John Keats's Dream of Truth* (1969)
Marjorie Levinson, *Keats's Life of Allegory* (1988)
K. Muir (ed.), *John Keats: A Reassessment* (1958)
Judith O'Neill (ed.), *Critics on Keats* (1967)
Christopher Ricks, *Keats and Embarrassment* (1974)
M. R. Ridley, *Keats' Craftsmanship* (1933)
Robert M. Ryan, *Keats: The Religious Sense* (1976)
Stuart M. Sperry, *Keats the Poet* (1973)
Jack Stillinger (ed.), *Keats's Odes: A Collection of Critical Essays* (1968)
——, *The Hoodwinking of Madeline* (1971)
Helen Vendler, *The Odes of John Keats* (1983)
William Walsh, *Introduction to Keats* (1981)
E. R. Wasserman, *The Finer Tone: Keats' Major Poems* (1953)
Susan Wolfson et al., 'Keats and Politics: A Forum', *Studies in Romanticism*, 25 (1986)

Shelley

Texts

There is at present no satisfactory standard edition of Shelley's complete works. The Longman 'Annotated English Poets' edition of the *Complete Poems*, edited by G. M. Matthews and Kelvin Everest, provides a reliable modern text of the poetry, arranged in chronological order and with full annotation for all poems. At present only volume one is available (1989); volumes two and three are scheduled for publication in 1993 and 1997. The first volume of the Longman edition includes an Introduction which surveys the history of the text of Shelley's poetry, and describes the characteristics of each of the major editions published since Shelley's death. The Oxford Standard Authors *Poetical Works*, ed. Thomas Hutchinson (1904, revised by G. M. Matthews, Oxford 1970), remains in the meantime the least unsatisfactory currently available text of Shelley's complete poetry.

Shelley's works in prose are currently being edited for Oxford University Press. Until the appearance of that scholarly edition the reader must rely on the relevant volumes of the 'Julian' edition of Shelley's works, edited by Roger Ingpen and Walter Peck (1926–30), or on David Lee Clark's collection *Shelley's Prose or The Trumpet of a Prophecy* (1954, corrected edn, 1967, new edn, 1988). Both of these collections, but more particularly Clark's, are extremely unreliable in their texts, datings and notes. They are also both far from complete. H. B. Forman's four-volume edition of 1880 is in many respects superior to any subsequent text, but it is not easy to find. Shelley's two youthful gothic novels, *Zastrozzi* and *St Irvyne*, are currently available in a World's Classics edition by Stephen C. Behrendt (1986).

The standard edition of Shelley's letters is *The Letters of Percy Bysshe Shelley*, ed. F. L. Jones (2 vols, Oxford, 1964). This too is an edition which has come to seem increasingly unsatisfactory. It omits a quite large number of the letters now known to survive, and makes more mistakes and modifications in the text than are acceptable by modern standards. Nevertheless, no new edition is currently planned.

Interested readers now have access to the exceptionally complex manuscript materials underlying many of Shelley's texts, by consulting the volumes in two scholarly series published by Garland, 'The Manuscripts of the Younger British Romantics' (including three volumes of Shelley material), and 'The Bodleian Shelley Manuscripts', both under the general editorship of Donald H. Reiman. A further rich source of information and commentary is the eight volumes so far published of *Shelley and his Circle*, eds Kenneth N. Cameron (vols 1–4, 1961–70) and Donald H. Reiman (Vols 5–8, 1973–86).

There are some good selections of Shelley's poetry. *Shelley's Poetry and Prose*, eds Donald H. Reiman and Sharon B. Powers (1977), is a very full selection with good texts, helpful notes, and an excellent annotated bibliography. It also includes two of Shelley's most important prose works, and a selection of critical essays on the poetry. Also recommended are the 'Everyman' *Selected Poems*, ed. Timothy Webb (1977), the New Oxford English Series *Selected Poems and Prose*, ed. G. M. Matthews (Oxford, 1964) and *Alastor, Prometheus Unbound, and Adonais*, ed. Peter Butter (1970). The notes in C. D. Locock's two-volume edition of the *Poems* (1911) are still worth consulting.

The standard scholarly biography is by Newman Ivey White, *Shelley* (2 vols, 1940), although this work is now in many respects out of date. Richard Holmes, *Shelley: The Pursuit* (1974) is lively, readable and well-informed, but it is unreliable in some of its critical and biographical judgements.

Criticism

Miriam Allott (ed.), *Essays on Shelley* (1982)
Carlos Baker, *Shelley's Major Poetry: The Fabric of a Vision* (1948)
Harold Bloom, *Shelley's Mythmaking* (1959)
Peter Butter, *Shelley's Idols of the Cave* (1954)
Kenneth Neill Cameron, *The Young Shelley: Genesis of a Radical* (1950)
——, *Shelley: The Golden Years* (1974)
Judith Chernaik, *The Lyrics of Shelley* (1972)
Timothy Clark, *Embodying Revolution: The Figure of the Poet in Shelley* (1989)
Richard Cronin, *Shelley's Poetic Thoughts* (1981)
Stuart Curran, *Shelley's 'Cenci': Scorpions Ringed with Fire* (1970)
——, *Shelley's Annus Mirabilis: The Maturing of an Epic Vision* (1975)
Paul Dawson, *The Unacknowledged Legislator: Shelley and Politics* (1983)

Kelvin Everest (ed.), *Shelley Revalued: Essays from the Gregynog Conference* (1983)
Paul Foot, *Red Shelley* (1980)
* Jerrold Hogle, *Shelley's Process: Radical Transference and the Development of his Major Works* (1989)
William Keach, *Shelley's Style* (1984)
Desmond King-Hele, *Shelley: His Thought and Work* (2nd edn, 1971)
Angela Leighton, *Shelley and the Sublime* (1984)
G. M. Matthews, *Shelley* (1970)
Michael O'Neill, *The Human Mind's Imaginings: Conflict and Achievement in Shelley's Poetry* (1989)
David B. Pirie, *Shelley* (1988)
C. E. Pulos, *The Deep Truth: A Study of Shelley's Scepticism* (1954)
Donald H. Reiman, *Percy Bysshe Shelley* (1969)
G. M. Ridenour (ed.), *Shelley: A Collection of Critical Essays* (1965)
Charles E. Robinson, *Shelley and Byron: The Snake and Eagle Wreathed in Fight* (1976)
Michael Scrivener, *Radical Shelley* (1982)
Stuart M. Sperry, *Shelley's Major Verse: The Narrative and Dramatic Poetry* (1988)
Patrick Swinden (ed.), *Shelley: Shorter Poems and Lyrics* (1976)
Earl R. Wasserman, *Shelley: A Critical Reading* (1971)
Timothy Webb, *Shelley: A Voice not Understood* (1977)
——, *The Violet in the Crucible: Shelley and Translation* (1976)
Milton Wilson, *Shelley's Later Poetry: A Study of his Prophetic Imagination* (1959)
R. B. Woodings (ed.), *Shelley: Modern Judgements* (1968)

Index

Abrams, M.H., 22
Anti-Jacobin, 58
Arnold, Matthew, 41
Austen, Jane, 28–9, 33, 34
  Mansfield Park, 30, 33, 55
  Pride and Prejudice, 30, 54–5
  Sense and Sensibility, 30, 54

Baillie, Joanna, 83
Barbauld, Anna Laetitia 4
Bentham, Jeremy, 37
Blackwood, William, 70, 73
Blackwood's Edinburgh Magazine, 71, 73, 82–5
Blake, William, 1, 3, 12, 20–1, 31, 32, 33, 37, 39, 48, 53–4, 56, 67–9
  'An Island in the Moon', 53
  Europe, 21
  Songs of Innocence and of Experience, 12, 28, 56, 67, 73
  The Book of Thel, 21
  'The Chimney Sweeper', 28
  'The Ecchoing Green', 28
  'The Lamb', 28
  The Marriage of Heaven and Hell, 2, 56
  Visions of the Daughters of Albion, 21

Boulton, Matthew, 55
Brummell, George 'Beau', 34
Burdett, Sir Francis, 63
Burke, Edmund, 11, 17–19, 25, 30, 76
  Letters on a Regicide Peace, 25
  Reflections on the Revolution in France, 18–19, 25, 30
Burns, Robert, 1, 83
Byron, George Gordon, Lord, 1, 3, 33, 43–5, 47, 48, 59–64, 70–1, 79, 80–2, 85
  Childe Harold's Pilgrimage, 60, 63, 70–1, 81
  Don Juan, 43–4, 63, 71, 82, 85
  English Bards and Scotch Reviewers, 62
  Lara, 71
  The Bride of Abydos, 71
  The Corsair, 71
  The Siege of Corinth, 71
  The Vision of Judgment, 73

Calderon, 5
Calvert, Raisley, 54
Campbell, Thomas, 1, 70
Castlereagh, Robert Stewart, Viscount, 43–5, 47
Charles II, 25

Index

Clare, John, 2
Cobbett, William, 19
Coleridge, Samuel Taylor, 1, 3, 12,
    19, 31, 32, 41, 48, 53–8, 60, 63,
    67, 68, 72, 80
  Biographia Literaria, 37, 78, 79–80
  Christabel, 80
  'Dejection Ode', 17
  'Destruction of the Bastille', 15
  'Frost at Midnight', 56
  The Ancient Mariner, 17, 58, 80
  'This Lime-Tree Bower my
    Prison', 56
Constable, Archibald, 70, 73
Cottle, Joseph, 67
Cowper, William, 1, 5, 18
Croker, John Wilson, 83

Dante, 5
Darwin, Erasmus, 1
De Quincey, Thomas, 74

Edinburgh Review, 62, 73–6
Eldon, John Scott, 1st Earl of, 45–6
Eliot, T.S., 41
Elizabeth I, 10
Examiner, 7, 82–3

Fox, Charles James, 15, 23

Galton, Samuel, 55
George III, 9, 16, 18
George IV (Prince Regent), 33, 82
Gifford, William, 62, 73–4, 83
Gillray, James, 23–8, 33
  'Promis'd Horrors of the French
    Invasion', 25
  'Smelling out a Rat', 25
  'The New Morality', 58
  'The Zenith of French Glory', 23
Gilpin, William, 10
Godwin, William, 19–20, 53, 55, 60
  Enquiry Concerning Political Justice,
    5, 53

Hardy, Thomas, 56
Haydon, Benjamin Robert, 84
Hazlitt, William, 74, 77–9
  Lectures on the English Poets, 77
  'On the Living Poets', 77–9
  The Spirit of the Age, 34, 69–70,
    77, 79
Holcroft, Thomas, 19, 53
Holland, Henry Richard Vassal Fox,
    3rd Baron, 61–2
Hunt, Leigh, 59, 74, 77, 82–5
Hunt, 'Orator' Henry, 45

James II, 14
Jeffrey, Francis, 73–7, 79
Johnson, Joseph, 53

Keats, John, 1, 3, 5, 33, 38–9,
    48–50, 59–60, 73, 77, 80–5
  Endymion, 82–4
  Isabella: or, the Pot of Basil, 49
  Lamia, 37–8
  'Ode to a Nightingale', 50, 60
  'Ode to Psyche', 39
  Poems (1817), 83
  The Eve of St Agnes, 49

Lackington, James, 69
Lamb, Charles, 58, 74
Leavis, F.R., 41
Liverpool, 2nd Earl of, 42
Lockhart, John Gibson, 83–5
London Magazine, 73–4, 85
Longman, Thomas, 70
Louis XVI, 30

Malthus, Thomas, 9–10
  *Essay on the Principle of
    Population*, 10
Marie-Antoinette, 30
Milton, John, 5
Moore, Thomas, 1, 70
  Lalla Rookh, 70
More, Hannah, 36
Morris, William, 49
Murray, John, 70, 73

Napoleon, 3, 31–2, 42, 62
Nelson, Horatio, Lord, 32
Newton, Isaac, 38
Nicholson, William, 68
Norfolk, Duke of, 60
Nottingham Review, 61

Ollier, Charles, 71

Paine, Thomas, 17–19, 53
  Common Sense, 18
  Rights of Man, 18–19, 72
Petrarch, 5
Pitt (the younger), William, 15, 23, 43
Poole, Tom, 54
Pope, Alexander, 62, 82, 84
Price, Dr Richard, 18, 25
Priestley, Joseph, 55

Quarterly Review, 62, 73–4, 82–5

Ricardo, David, 36
Robespierre, Maximilien, 30
Rogers, Samuel, 1, 70
Rousseau, Jean-Jacques, 5

Scott, John, 73–4, 85
Scott, Sir Walter, 1, 70
  Marmion, 70
  The Lady of the Lake, 70
Shakespeare, William, 1
Shelley, Mary, 21
  Frankenstein, 21
Shelley, Percy Bysshe, 1, 3, 5, 21, 33, 38–41, 43–8, 59, 60, 63–4, 70–2, 80–3
  Adonais, 85
  Alastor, 71, 81
  'England in 1819', 33–4
  Laon and Cythna, 21, 71
  'Ode to Heaven', 72
  'Ode to Liberty', 44
  'Ode to the West Wind', 72
  Peter Bell the Third, 80–1

Prometheus Unbound, 21, 30–1, 38–40, 44, 71–2
The Mask of Anarchy, 45–6, 71, 73
The Revolt of Islam, 21, 71
'To a Sky-Lark', 72
'To the Republic of Benevento', 44
Sidmouth, Henry Addington, 1st Viscount, 45–6
Smith, Adam, 36
Smith, Charlotte, 4
Southey, Robert, 41, 58, 74, 75–6, 78, 83
  Letters from England, 11–12, 41
  Thalaba, 75
Spence, Thomas, 55

Taylor, Jane, 4
Thelwall, John, 19, 53
Thompson, E.P., 49
Thomson, James, 5
Times, 68

Walker, Adam, 40
Watt, James, 55
Wedgwood, Josiah, 54
Wesley, John, 34, 36
Wilberforce, William, 36
Wilkes, John, 16
William of Orange, 14
Wollstonecraft, Mary, 19–20, 53
  Vindication of the Rights of Women, 19–20
Wordsworth, Dorothy, 58
Wordsworth, William, 1, 3, 5, 12–14, 19, 31, 32, 33, 48–9, 53–8, 60, 63, 67, 68, 75–82
  Lyrical Ballads, 2, 58, 67, 73, 75–80, 82, 84–5
  Poems in Two Volumes, 77
  Preface to *Lyrical Ballads*, 37, 76–7, 82
  The Excursion, 12, 33, 77–8, 79, 81
  The Prelude, 12–14, 48–9, 58
  'The Recluse', 12